Charlie Greenleaf

The politics surrounding the use of urban space exposes the interaction of economic, physical, social, and political factors that shape contemporary society. This exposure is especially revealing when focused on a single community during a period of dramatic transformation. *Money Sings* explores the sweeping reorganization of Russian life during the initial post-Soviet era (August 1991–December 1993) by examining the politics of property in a Russian "Middletown," the historic industrial city of Yaroslavl.

Located on the banks of the Volga 150 miles northeast of Moscow, post-Soviet Yaroslavl reveals what can happen to a city when money suddenly takes on meaning. Bureaucratic battles over property, plans for automobile suburbs to be built on collective farms, major court battles, discredited local officials, and environmental disasters add texture to abstract notions about transitions to a market economy and political democracy. The politics of urban space—what a city looks like and how it functions—explodes in Yaroslavl as local officials wrest power from central authorities and those who control money subvert formal planning procedures that once favored privilege and bureaucratic status. This volume, which details housing privatization, historic preservation, and urban planning, demonstrates important lessons about the bureaucratic and political dynamics of systemic change in post-Soviet Russia, the economic transition to the market, and the importance of economic factors in shaping the contemporary city.

South view, Church of the Archangel Michael. Photograph by William C. Brumfield.

WOODROW WILSON CENTER SERIES

Money sings

Other books in the series

Michael J. Lacey, editor, *Religion and Twentieth-Century American Intellectual Life*

Michael J. Lacey, editor, *The Truman Presidency*

Joseph Kruzel and Michael H. Haltzel, editors, *Between the Blocs: Problems and Prospects for Europe's Neutral and Nonaligned States*

William C. Brumfield, editor, *Reshaping Russian Architecture: Western Technology, Utopian Dreams*

Mark N. Katz, editor, *The USSR and Marxist Revolutions in the Third World*

Walter Reich, editor, *Origins of Terrorism: Psychologies, Ideologies, Theologies, States of Mind*

Mary O. Furner and Barry Supple, editors, *The State and Economic Knowledge: The American and British Experiences*

Michael J. Lacey and Knud Haakonssen, editors, *A Culture of Rights: The Bill of Rights in Philosophy, Politics, and Law—1791 and 1991*

Robert J. Donovan and Ray Scherer, *Unsilent Revolution: Television News and American Public Life, 1948–1991*

Nelson Lichtenstein and Howell John Harris, editors, *Industrial Democracy in America: The Ambiguous Promise*

William Craft Brumfield and Blair A. Ruble, editors, *Russian Housing in the Modern Age: Design and Social History*

Michael J. Lacey and Mary O. Furner, editors, *The State and Social Investigation in Britain and the United States*

Hugh Ragsdale, editor, *Imperial Russian Foreign Policy*

Dermot Keogh and Michael H. Haltzel, editors, *Northern Ireland and the Politics of Reconciliation*

Joseph Klaits and Michael H. Haltzel, editors, *The Global Ramifications of the French Revolution*

René Lemarchand, *Burundi: Ethnocide as Discourse and Practice*

James R. Millar and Sharon L. Wolchik, editors, *The Social Legacy of Communism*

James M. Morris, editor, *On Mozart*

Theodore Taranovski, editor, *Reform in Modern Russian History: Progress or Cycle?*

Money sings

The changing politics of urban space in post-Soviet Yaroslavl

Blair A. Ruble

WOODROW WILSON CENTER PRESS

AND

Published by the Press Syndicate of the University of Cambridge
The Pitt Building, Trumpington Street, Cambridge CB2 1RP
40 West 20th Street, New York, NY 10011-4211, USA
10 Stamford Road, Oakleigh, Melbourne 3166, Australia

First published 1995

Printed in the United States of America

Library of Congress Cataloging-in-Publication Data
Ruble, Blair A., 1949–
Money sings: the changing politics of urban space in post-Soviet
Yaroslavl / Blair A. Ruble.
p. cm.—(Woodrow Wilson Center series)
Includes bibliographical references and index.
ISBN 0-521-48242-9
1. City planning—Russia (Federation)—Iaroslavl' (Iaroslavskaia
oblast') 2. Historic preservation—Russia (Federation)—Iaroslavl'
(Iaroslavskaia oblast') 3. Housing policy—Russia (Federation)—
Iaroslavl' (Iaroslavskaia oblast') 4. Iaroslavl' (Iaroslavskaia
oblast', Russia)—Economic conditions. 5. Post-communism—Russia
(Federation)—Iaroslavl' (Iaroslavskaia oblast') I. Title.
II. Series.
HT169.R82I167 1995
307.1'2'0947—dc20 94-40751
CIP

A catalog record for this book is available from the British Library.

ISBN 0–521–48242–9 hardback

U nas den'gi ne govoriat, den'gi poiut!
(Here, money does not talk, money sings!)

Contents

Figures and tables

TABLES

Preface

Somewhat over a decade ago, the Institute for Governmental Studies of the University of California at Berkeley invited me to write a volume on the governing of Leningrad for the Franklin K. Lane Studies Series on Regional Governance. This invitation eventually led to the publication of *Leningrad: Shaping a Soviet City* in 1990.

On receiving the institute's invitation, I immediately set out to discover what I could about the city. Having lived in Leningrad, I thought I knew the town rather well. Unfortunately, I had failed to appreciate how little information was available about the place. Many of the data that analysts in the West would normally consult about economic, social, and political urban development were classified. Now that Leningrad has become St. Petersburg, and archives and planning offices are open to Western specialists, I understand that even those data that did exist might not have been of much assistance. Soviet officials did not always collect data similar to those gathered by their Western counterparts; or, if they did, dissimilar categories and headings were frequently employed. Even now, a researcher must approach a post-Soviet Russian city with more than the normal amount of caution. It is still as important as ever to think creatively about the data problem.

In pursuing my investigation of Leningrad's development, I began to draw on the physical city itself as a text for political analysis. Information on employment patterns may have been concealed and politicians may have been reluctant to speak to foreign researchers, but one could still walk the streets of Leningrad—at least, most of them—and look around. Such an approach would not have been at all unusual in such fields as urban history, urban geography, or urban planning. But political scientists have not attempted to draw on the physical contours of urban space for information about how urban politics works. Political scientists in the United States and Europe simply had no reason even to try to do so. When analysis demanded information, the Western investigator merely turned to official data, surveys, or interviews. By contrast, with the interest taken by the Leningrad administration of the KGB in my own research, I was forced to seek surrogate sources of information, and in so doing, I discovered the physical texture of the city as a valuable resource for understanding Leningrad's economic, social, and even political development. I began to appreciate just how much we can learn about the who, what, where, when, why, and how of urban politics from the very stones of a city.

I remain convinced that a city's physical development contains important clues to its political life, especially in post-Soviet Russia. Local archives are opening up across Russia, public opinion polls can be carried out for the right price, and politicians are more than happy to grant interviews. Yet many critical decisions are not contained in the chronicles of an archive. Public opinion remains too volatile to be a reliable guide to the overall course of events. Politicians and other officials have themselves changed so much in recent years that they too are often unable to recount Soviet-era events accurately. In short, additional data are required to make sense of the current bedlam that is Russian political life.

I should like to propose that political disputes surrounding changes in a city's physical structure offer valuable insights into contemporary Russian politics. This is nowhere more the case than in urban communities, where so much of the tumult of the Gorbachev and post-Soviet eras has been played out.

There are two particularly sweeping transitions among the transformations that are occurring simultaneously in Russia today: one from a totalitarian-oriented political system, the other from a centrally administered economic system. The ultimate destinations of these journeys remain very much in doubt at this writing. In both cases, the who, what, where, when, why, and how of politics are all undergoing profound changes. By focusing on the policy issues surrounding the physical development of a single provincial city—on the politics of housing privatization, historic preservation, and land use in the Volga town of Yaroslavl—I hope to be able to shed light on both the emergence of the post-Soviet city and the reform process itself. I seek to define the socialist nature of Yaroslavl and other Soviet-era Russian cities in the pages that follow and to chart the dramatic transformations that are accompanying the broadening of political life and the introduction of market relations into the economy.

Most readers probably will conclude that my accomplishments in this volume are rather modest. I pose far more questions than I am able to answer; I offer only incomplete impressions where in-depth detail may be demanded; I include few numbers for quantitative analysis. I provide, in short, a Polaroid snapshot when a portrait in oil may be preferred.

My only defense against such charges is that the transitions in Yaroslavl—as in all of Russia—are moving so swiftly that the subject does not as yet lend itself to formal portraiture. The December 1993 parliamentary elections and constitutional referendum marked the end of Russia's first post-Soviet republic. Nevertheless, the situation has continued to change. Yaroslavl life will be substantially different by the time the first reader sees this sentence in print. Modest snapshots have a value in such a fickle season, especially for historians from some distant future who will begin to read the outcome of Russia's current *smuta* (time of troubles) back onto today's events. Meanwhile, observers of the contemporary Russian scene must settle for posing questions that may reveal but tiny portions of the dramatically new landscape that is just now taking shape.

Many questions emerge from my conversations and my observations during seven visits to Yaroslavl between June 1990 and September 1993—a period that roughly corresponds to Russia's first post-Soviet republic, headed by President Boris Yeltsin. A list of my more formal meetings with Yaroslavtsy and others may be found in the Selected Bibliography. These sessions do not exhaust the extent of my encounters in the city, however. I also had several meetings with Yaroslavtsy in Moscow, Washington, D.C., and elsewhere. This list merely chronicles those moments when everyone understood that they were speaking "for the record."

I have come to consider many of my Yaroslavl interlocutors as something more than mere objects for social science investigation. I found these women and men to be struggling with much honor and no little dignity to come to terms with a world in turmoil—a world for which they could never have been prepared. It is easy to become cynical about the motives of politicians in any country, let alone in the chaotic Russia of the early 1990s. Nonetheless, I am compelled to observe that nearly all of the sixty-odd officials interviewed for this study aspired to act in a manner that would advance the interests of their community. I have sought—even at moments of disagreement or disapproval—to treat these "subjects" with the fairness, honesty, and respect they most certainly deserve.

If I have been successful, this study will reveal something to the reader about the post-Soviet transition not just in Yaroslavl but in Russia more generally. It may also demonstrate the ways in which an examination of disputes over physical urban space can provide information for political analysis. My rather minimalist intent is that the pages that follow will begin to interest political scientists in a new source for useful insights into the political process, a source composed, quite literally, of the stones, cement, and glass that surround them every day.

I should note at this point that I have relied on the Library of Congress system of transliteration of Russian into English, except in the case of commonly Anglicized names. This exception has singular significance for this particular work because it has led me to transliterate in the text—but not in the footnote citations—the name of the subject community as Yaroslavl rather than as the more precise Iaroslavl'.

In closing, I should like to express my gratitude to the Carnegie Corporation of New York for providing the financial support that made this study possible. In addition, I should like to express heartfelt thanks to my Moscow colleagues Vsevolod Vasil'ev, Mikhail Marchenko, and the late, much missed Georgii Barabashev for their support. My American colleagues Jo Andrews, Timothy Colton, Jeffrey Hahn, Henry Hale, Jerry Hough, Lolly Jewitt, Susan Lehmann, and Kathryn Stoner-Weiss are to be credited for intellectual guidance. Tatiana Pavlovna Rumiantseva, of Yaroslavl, deserves special acknowledgment for her energetic and steadfast encouragement of my research efforts as well as for her unflappable good humor. Matt Keough and Susanna Bolle, Kennan Institute interns, were very helpful in assisting with the preparation of this manuscript. Todd Weinberg, Annemarie Wollam, and Galina Levina, of New Europe Associates (Moscow), provided invaluable logistical support. William Craft Brumfield generously granted permission to include several of his elegant architectural photographs in this volume. Most important, Edward Bergman, Pavel Il'yn, Aleksandr Khodnev, Patricia Kolb, Leonard Plotnicov, Hank Savitch, Steven Solnick, Joseph Tulchin, and various anonymous readers, together with the participants at several seminars and conference panels[1] (especially at my graduate alma mater, the University of Toronto), offered sharp criticisms and perceptive comments that, I hope, have improved this study during its several revisions.

[1]Earlier versions of this study were presented at various conferences, in the following papers: "Novyi oblik goroda: politika sobstvennosti v Iaroslavle," *Mezhdunarodnaia nauchno-prakticheskaia konferentsiia: Predstavitel'nye organy mestnogo samoupravleniia v sovremennom mire*, Iaroslavl', R.F. (27–28 aprelia 1992 goda); "Okhrana istoricheskogo naslediia, chastnaia sobstvennost', i ekonomicheskoe razvitie: konkuriruiushchie ili dopolniaiushchie tseli v Rossii?," *Mezhdunarodnaia konferentsiia po istorii gorodskoi sredy i sotsial'no-kul'turnoi politike*, Moscow, R.F. (24–29 avgusta 1992 goda); "A Case Study in Policy Making: Urban Planning in Iaroslavl'," Conference on Democratization in Russia: The Development of Legislative Institutions, Harvard University, Cambridge, Mass. (October 29–30, 1993); "The Politics of Property in Iaroslavl'," American Association for the Advancement of Slavic Studies National Meeting, Honolulu, Hawaii (November 15, 1993). Sections have also appeared in print as the following works: "Iaroslavl' in Russia: Learning the Politics of Compromise," *Woodrow Wilson Center Report* 2, no. 2 (1990): 14–15; "Living without Institutions," *New Outlook* 3, nos. 1–2 (1992): 7–9; "Narisuem—budem zhit'?," *Severnyi krai* (Iaroslavl'), August 21, 1992, p. 2; "Reshaping the City: The Politics of Property in a Provincial Russian City," *Urban Anthropology* 21, no. 3 (1992); "Novyi oblik goroda: politika sobstvennosti v Iaroslavle," in Iaroslavskii gorodskoi sovet narodnykh deputatov i Tsentr izucheniia obshchestvennogo mneniia i sotsiologicheskikh issledovanii "TsIOMSI," *Mezhdunarodnaia nauchno-prakticheskaia konferentsiia: Predstavitel'nye organy mestnogo samoupravleniia v sovremennom mire. Doklady. Tezisy vystuplenii, materialy diskussii (27–28 aprelia 1992 goda)* (Iaroslavl': Iaroslavskii gorodskoi sovet narodnykh deputatov, 1993), pp. 95–125; "From *Khrushcheby* to *Korobki*," in William C. Brumfield and Blair A. Ruble, eds., *Russian Housing in the Modern Age* (Cambridge: Cambridge University Press, 1993), pp. 232–70; "A Strange Village from Another Galaxy: From Moscow to Yaroslavl' and Back," *Woodrow Wilson Center Report* 5, no. 2 (1993): 12–14; "Rossiiskie reformy i okhrana istoricheskikh pamiatnikov v provintsial'nom gorode," in O. G. Sevan, ed., *Sotsiokul'turnoe obosnovanie formirovaniia predmetno-prostranstvennoi sredy goroda (po materialam mezhdunarodnogo soveshchaniia "Istoricheskaia gorodskaia sreda i sotsiokul'turnaia politika")* (Moscow: Rossiiskii institut kul'turologii, forthcoming).

Introduction:
The politics of property in
a provincial Russian city

The meeting was clandestine, arranged by go-betweens who insisted on remaining anonymous. His body conformed more easily to those old cheap gray Communist Party suits of the past than to his new sleek German threads. His breath reeked of garlic and onions. So this was one of the "New Russians," the shady entrepreneurs who had manipulated the uncertainties of the Soviet Union's collapse for enormous personal gain. He dealt in futures of a sort, buying up newly privatized apartments from pensioners in exchange for modest supplements to their monthly support payments from an increasingly bankrupt state. When asked what differences there were in urban development under the Soviet and the post-Soviet regimes, he switched conspiratorially to the familiar second-person singular: *"Kak amerikanets,* as an American, *ty eto khorosho ponimaesh,* you understand this very well. You Americans have an expression, *'Den'gi poiut,'* 'Money sings.' That explains all." On learning that money in America talks rather than sings, he responded, "Well, we Russians have always been more extravagant."

Order within a city results from the accumulation of layer upon layer of social, economic, cultural, and political sediment. The very shape of a city, the use of its land, the style of its buildings, and the nature of its infrastructure reveal a great deal about the society that creates and inhabits it. Shifting architectural and urban patterns exemplify a society's ability to adapt to technological, social, economic, and even political change. Urban vistas express the manner in which societies function and think about themselves.

1

The texture of a city divulges inside information about power relations in a given society. Which institutions occupy central space: government buildings, military bodies, churches, banks, shopping centers? Which are relegated to the periphery of a city? Indeed, is the "center" of urban life even central, or has it shifted to the periphery to form an "edge city"?[1] Who owns land and buildings: individuals, corporations, the state? Who are neighbors? Do land-use patterns encode socioeconomic segregation, ethnic cleavages, institutional allegiances, or professional ties? Are these decisions determined by the "invisible hand" of the market or by the conspicuous hand of the bureaucratic state? The answers to these questions, especially at the micro level of daily existence, expose core issues of politics revolving around precisely who gets what.[2] These transactions emerge in sharpest relief at those moments when the very mechanisms for determining society's winners and losers undergo rapid and thoroughgoing transmutation.

The sweeping reorganization of Russian social, political, and economic organization during the post-Soviet period dramatically alters entrenched patterns in urban life. Physical change occurs in the organization of a city as private property is introduced, passing land and buildings from state monopolies to individual and corporate ownership. The desire of individuals and corporate organizations to own and control their own small corner of the city encourages rapid decentralization and urban sprawl. Social differentiation and fragmentation may also increase as market mechanisms take hold. New cleavages generate previously unknown—or at least submerged—conflicts and competitions, which require vigorous institutional and political responses. Local communities struggle to devise fresh institutional structures and mechanisms for managing conflict. These processes are altering the distribution of urban political and economic power throughout post-Soviet Russia.

An analysis of the politics of urban space in a single community at the outset of the post-Soviet transition promises to expose the interaction of the economic, physical, social, and political factors that shape the contemporary city. This study begins to explore these dynamic relation-

[1] Many observers of the American urban scene have commented on the transfer of urban life to the edge of cities. Among the more popular discussions of this phenomenon are Robert Fishman, "Megalopolis Unbound," *Wilson Quarterly* 14 (1990): 25–45, and Joel Garreau, *Edge City: Life on the New Frontier* (New York: Doubleday, 1991).

[2] An interesting discussion of these issues in relation to Moscow may be found in O. E. Trushchenko, "Akkumuliatsiia simvolicheskogo kapitala v prostranstve stolichnogo tsentra," *Rossiiskii monitor,* vyp. 3 (1993), pp. 145–65.

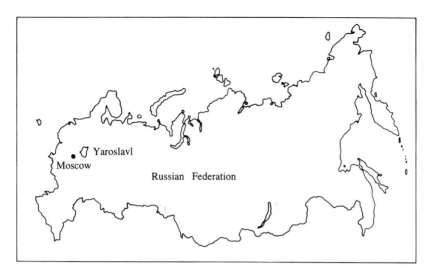

Figure 1. Map of the Russian Federation showing the relationship of Yaroslavl to Moscow.

ships through an examination of changes in the physical structures and organizational forms of a single Russian city—Yaroslavl—over the period encompassing Mikhail Gorbachev's vaunted perestroika (restructuring) policies of the late 1980s and Russia's first post-Soviet republic of Boris Yeltsin's presidency (August 1991–December 1993).

YAROSLAVL AS ''MIDDLETOWN''

Yaroslavl (or, as it sometimes appears in English, Iaroslavl') was founded in 1010 at the confluence of the Volga and Kotorosl' rivers some 150 miles northeast of Moscow (Figures 1 and 2). Its current population is approximately 640,000, spread out along the banks of the Volga for nearly 50 miles (Figure 3).

The city is the capital of the Yaroslavl Oblast (Region), which is home to some one and one-half million residents—including those of the city of Yaroslavl. The region generally lies between the Volga River running from the northwest to the southeast and the Moscow Region to the south and west. The region's employment patterns remain fairly typical for Russian provinces as a whole (Table 1).

In addition to the city of Yaroslavl, the region includes the industrial

Figure 2. Map showing the relationship of the city of Yaroslavl to the Yaroslavl Region and surrounding regions.

city of Rybinsk as well as the historic towns of Rostov-Veliki, Uglich, Pereslavl-Zalesski, and Tutaev. Predominantly agricultural, such rural areas traditionally were home to flax and dairy production. Much of the area's most productive land was submerged under the Rybinsk reservoir, which formed during the 1940s after the completion of a major hydro-electric station.

Yaroslavl's economy evolved over the centuries, moving the city from a reliance on trade and handicrafts to its emergence as a significant man-ufacturing center after the completion of a major rail line to Moscow in

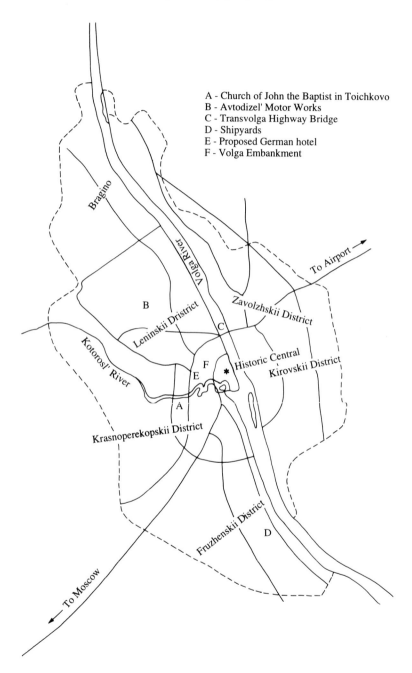

A - Church of John the Baptist in Toichkovo
B - Avtodizel' Motor Works
C - Transvolga Highway Bridge
D - Shipyards
E - Proposed German hotel
F - Volga Embankment

Figure 3. Map of Yaroslavl.

Table 1. *Employment by economic sector, 1990 (percent)*

Sector	Yaroslavl Region	Average for six surrounding regions[a]	Central Russia	Russian Federation
Agriculture & Forestry	9.8	10.0	11.4	12.2
Industry & Construction	51.4	47.5	43.1	43.4
Transport & Trade	14.1	13.8	14.7	16.0
Other (Including Services)	24.7	28.7	30.8	28.4

[a]Moscow (minus Moscow City), Tver, Vologda, Kostroma, Ivanovo, and Vladimir regions
Source: Andrei Treivish, "Tipichnyi krizis v tipichnom regione," *Vash vybor*, 1993, no. 1, pp. 12–13.

1870.[3] The first Russian automobile—the "Lebed'" (Swan)—was sched-uled to have rolled off a Yaroslavl assembly line in 1917.[4] That effort collapsed in the chaos of the Bolshevik Revolution and the Civil War. The local economy nonetheless came to rely heavily on major factories connected with the automotive industry, including Russia's most impor-tant diesel motor, tire, and auto-paint factories, as well as a major oil refinery.

Yaroslavl remains fairly atypical for a Russian city of its size in one way that is rather helpful for this particular study. Unlike towns located farther west and south, Yaroslavl was essentially untouched by World War II. The town certainly suffered greatly during the Russian Civil War (1918–21), and a few German bombing raids were directed at local fac-tories and railyards. Stalinist industrialization policies and later inatten-tion to historical monuments also took their toll on the Yaroslavl townscape. Yet, it is far more possible to read the city's history in its physical structure than is the case in many other provincial Russian cities of similar size and significance. The elemental character of a pre-Soviet trading town still defines the city core. A Stalinist "rust belt" factory town belches pollution nearby, while Brezhnev-era blighted moonscapes delimit newer districts farther away from downtown. A distinctive phys-

[3]Andrei Kuz'michev and Igor' Shapkin, "Delovoi Iaroslavl'," *Vash vybor*, 1993, no. 1, pp. 18–21.
[4]Ibid.

ical text endures, providing inestimable clues to nearly a millennium of habitation.

LOCAL VARIATIONS ON NATIONAL POLITICAL THEMES

Governmental structures and procedures at the local level have remained erratic as today's community leaders jostle for political and economic advantage. Tensions between popularly elected legislative agencies—the *sovety*—and bureaucratically entrenched executive committees—the *ispolkomy*—forced the wholesale reorganization of municipal governance in the wake of the Soviet Union's 1991 disintegration.[5] Such skirmishes spawned dozens of governing coalitions and alliances, which varied from one moment and one locale to the next. If local conflicts have not sufficiently intensified development and planning decisions on their own, the continuing battles in Moscow between the national parliament and the executive branch also reverberate throughout Russian regional and municipal political life. This confusion became especially pronounced during the months leading up to the tragic showdown between Parliament and the president around the Moscow "White House" on October 3–4, 1993.

In Yaroslavl, local politics were compounded by the failure of either the established Communist political machine or the nascent democratic opposition to secure a clear-cut victory in the March 1990 elections to both the regional—oblast—and the city councils. The city had had a reputation during the late 1980s for being one of the more radical, democratically oriented communities in all of the Soviet Union (Figure 4).[6] This activism led Nikolai Travkin, Georgi Khatsenkov, and chess grand master Garri Kasparov to convene the August 1990 founding assembly of their Democratic Party of Russia in Yaroslavl.[7] That party, in turn, had grown out of the success of several regional "people's fronts" (na-

---

[5] Andrei Pokhmelkin and Viktor Pokhmelkin, "Zakon protiv traditsii," *Vash vybor,* 1992, no. 11, pp. 8–10.

[6] See, for example, such press articles as the following: Michael Dobbs, "In Yaroslavl, Perestroika Brings Only More Hardship," *Washington Post,* November 7, 1989, pp. A1, A20; Peter Gumbel, "Soviet Elections Promise Big Changes," *Wall Street Journal,* February 23, 1990, p. A8; Dmitry Kazutin, "Rumours and Newspapers," *Moscow News Weekly,* 1990, no. 19, p. 5; and Pavel Nikitin, "Iaroslavskii barometr," *Ogonek,* 1990, no. 26, pp. 9–11.

[7] Pilar Bonet, *Figures in a Red Landscape,* trans. Norman Thomas di Giovanni and Susan Ashe (Washington, D.C.: Woodrow Wilson Center Press; Baltimore: Johns Hopkins University Press, 1993), pp. 41–51.

Figure 4. June 1990 meeting of the Yaroslavl People's Front. Photograph by Blair A. Ruble.

rodnye fronty), including an especially vibrant movement in Yaroslavl. Yet, apathy had settled in even before the 1990 elections could be held. As Spanish journalist Pilar Bonet reported, "From the vantage point of 1990, the 1987 Popular [People's] Front successes, which brought thousands out into the streets in protest against the Communist party decisions and rejected its provincial leaders, seemed insignificant alongside the fact that the reins of power remained in Communist hands."[8]

The March 1990 elections, which were perhaps the most open and competitive in the city's history, resulted in a "split decision" at both the regional and the city level.[9] In a pattern repeated in numerous Russian provinces, a free-floating coalition of the center emerged, which drifted with the passage of time to the "right" (away from market reforms and political democratization) at the regional level and to the "left" (toward market reforms and political democratization) within the city of Yaroslavl itself. As elsewhere in Russia, local Yaroslavl political life remained clouded also by unresolved rivalries between region and city and between legislature and executive.

By early 1992, executive authority in Yaroslavl had been consolidated in a new "regional administration" at the oblast level and a strengthened "mayor's office" in town. Symbolically, the mayor's office remained housed in the old city hall, which has served municipal administrators for well over a century, back into the late Imperial period (Figure 5). Unwieldy regional and city soviets—or councils—ceded legislative power at about the same time to newly created "mini-councils" *(malye sovety)* elected from among the deputies themselves. At the city level, 189 soviet deputies elected 16 of their peers to this new "small soviet."[10] The membership of the new council more or less conformed to the existing political, geographic, and bureaucratic balance of power found within the larger city council. City Council Chair Lev Kruglikov and Vice-Chair Vladimir Bakaev presided over both bodies.

The city council's mini-council continued to meet after the White

---

[8]Ibid., p. 44.

[9]The results and impact of the 1990 elections to the Yaroslavl City Soviet are discussed in Jeffrey W. Hahn, "Local Politics and Political Power in Russia: The Case of Yaroslavl'," *Soviet Economy* 7, no. 4 (1991): 322–41. The results and impact of the 1990 elections to the regional soviet are discussed in Jeffrey W. Hahn and Gavin Helf, "Old Dogs and New Tricks: Party Elites in the Russian Regional Elections of 1990," *Slavic Review* 51, no. 3 (Fall 1992): 511–30.

[10]Malyi sovet Iaroslavskogo gorodskogo soveta narodnykh deputatov, "Reshenie No. 4 o poriadke doizbraniia malogo Soveta gorodskogo Soveta narodnykh deputatov" (January 23, 1992).

Figure 5. The Yaroslavl city hall. Photograph by Blair A. Ruble.

House insurrection of October 3–4, 1993, in Moscow, but could no longer approve legislation. Its role was reduced to a consultative one, merely recommending actions to Yaroslavl Mayor Viktor Volonchunas.[11] Regional Council Deputy Chair Iulis Kolbovskii, a mathematician turned reform-oriented politician, was calm and self-assured as he discussed the initial refusal of the region's mini-council to disband itself. "I did all that was possible," he declared in an October 13, 1993, interview that appeared in the local youth paper *Iunost' (Youth)* three days later.[12] All attempts to protect the local soviets collapsed after President Yeltsin's subsequent announcement that the entire system of *sovety*, or councils, would be dismantled.[13] In an irony much commented on by the local press, the Yaroslavl Regional Council disbanded on the seventy-sixth

---

[11]Information obtained from Yaroslavl officials by Jeffrey Hahn of Villanova University through telephone conversations on October 25, 1993.

[12]The full interview appeared in Sergei Beliakov, "Iulis Kolbovskii: 'Vse, chto mozhno bylo, ia delal'," *Iunost'*, October 16, 1993, p. 1, and was reported later in I. Khrupalova, "Koridori vlasti: NaSovetovalis'? . . . ," *Severnyi krai*, October 27, 1993, pp. 1, 3.

[13]Ivan Rodin, "Sovetskaia predstavitel'naia vlast' polnost'iu likvidirovna," *Nezavisimaia gazeta*, October 28, 1993, p. 1.

anniversary of the opening of the Bolsheviks' very first Yaroslavl Provincial Congress of Soviets on October 27, 1917.[14] In discussing the collapse of the city council, Chair Kruglikov declared, "We leave with honor and have no need for personal recriminations."[15] By month's end, all Yaroslavl *sovety*—regional, city, and district, large and small—simply ceased to exist. Regional power came to rest in the hands of the chief of the Yaroslavl Regional Administration—the provincial "governor," as he became called in popular parlance—Anatolii Lisitsyn and his deputies; municipal power fell to Mayor Volonchunas and his team.[16]

URBAN POLICY DISPUTES IN RUSSIA'S UNCERTAIN TIMES

Despite the collapse of municipal administration at the end of the first post-Soviet republic, it is important to recall that the local government in Yaroslavl had gained a modicum of clarity during the early months of 1992. Subsequent struggles for national power between President Yeltsin and the Russian Federation Congress of People's Deputies—rather than local conflicts—later muddied the political waters. National policies emanating from Moscow continued to baffle all but the most cynical observer. Land laws failed to define precise procedures for resolving competing claims to title, so that innovative housing projects crumbled under a cloud of bribes, illegal auctions, squatters, and land grabs.[17] In major cities such as Moscow and St. Petersburg, mayors and city councils pursued their own contradictory housing privatization policies.[18] These skirmishes—when multiplied by a factor of some hundreds—reflect the chaos of urban administration during the first republic.

---

[14] I. Kopylova, "27.10.93g., 10 chas. 07 min.: sovetskaia vlast' v Iaroslavle prekratila techenie svoe (pochti po Saltykovu-Shchedrinu)" *Severnyi krai*, October 29, 1993, p. 1; Glava administratsii Iaroslavskoi oblasti, "Postanovlenie No. 273, 27.10.93, 'O reforme organa predstavitel'noi vlasti Iaroslavskoi oblasti,' " *Severnyi krai*, October 30, 1993, p. 1; and A. Pushkarnaia, "Iaroslavskii malyi gorsovet: segodnia my znaem, kto est' kto," *Severnyi krai*, October 30, 1993, p. 1.

[15] Pushkarnaia, "Iaroslavskii malyi gorsovet."

[16] Interview, Tatiana Pavlovna Rumiantseva, Director, Yaroslavl City Sociological Center, Washington, D.C., November 10, 1993.

[17] O. Z. Kaganova, "One-Family Housing Allotment: Legal Guarantee, Present Status in St. Petersburg and in the Region, Draft of Reforms and Analysis" (report prepared for the Urban Institute, Washington, D.C., January–March 1992), p. 4.

[18] Ibid., p. 6; Steve Erlanger, "In St. Petersburg, a Fight over Power and Property," *New York Times*, April 27, 1992, p. A3.

The continuing uncertainty surrounding urban and land policy in Russia—even after the bloody parliamentary insurrection of October 1993[19]—fostered several interrelated issues that blend into a single policy cluster revolving around the precise form and character of the urban future. Russians are using the pretext of the end of Soviet-style socialism to reimagine their towns and cities, with conflicts arising over procedures for privatizing housing, policies governing historic preservation, and land-use decision-making. Disputes over the shape of the Russian city have radiated out from central executive and legislative agencies in Moscow to confront municipal and enterprise officials, professionals, and citizens across the country's entire domain. Some managers and politicians yearn for recentralization, whereas other specialists demand the transfer of city-building authority to Russia's multifaceted regions. The future configuration and function of the Russian town in general—and of Yaroslavl in particular—will be determined by the ultimate resolution of the politics of urban space in the post-Soviet city.

YAROSLAVL LESSONS FOR REFORM IN RUSSIA

Emotional and divisive debates have swirled around the question of "reform" in Russia ever since Gorbachev launched perestroika in the mid-1980s. Commentators and politicians both in Russia and in the West have advocated the attachment of "fast," "slow," "systemic," "pragmatic," "top-down," "bottom-up," and any number of other adjectives to the golden word *reform*. In the West, adjectival preference frequently appears to be driven by disciplinary and philosophical concerns. Economists tend to favor quicker reform, arguing that speed will minimize the pain of systemic transition from a central planning to a market-oriented economic life. Commentators concerned with the anguish and political volatility of social dislocation argue that more time will be required to turn as large and complex a society as Russia in a new direction. Viewed from afar, it appeared that a grand social experiment was launched once again in Russia, with politicians and academics intent on imposing personal theories onto an economic, political, and social landscape already strewn with the wreckage of visionary and illusory schemes from centuries past.

Such debates are inevitable and necessary. Yet, their participants—be

[19]Oleg Polukeev, "Velikaia zemel'naia reforma?," *Nezavisimaia gazeta*, October 29, 1993, p. 1.

they Russian politicians, Moscow intellectuals, or Western scholars and journalists—have demonstrated only the most shadowy appreciation of precisely how various government policies supportive or antithetical to reform were actually shaping the lives of millions of individual Russians who live outside the Moscow Ring Road. Advocates of comprehensive reform strategies—be they fast or slow, top-down or bottom-up—have not always bothered to find out what the upheavals of the past five to ten years have meant for individual Russians. Provincial and city politicians, in contrast, have no choice but to respond to local conditions. One of the lessons of this study, then, will be that only local officials can turn policy pronouncement into local reality, since it is they who must try to square the circle between abstract economic models and everyday life.

CAPITALIST AND SOCIALIST URBAN DEVELOPMENT

This study also explores the differences between the capitalist and the Soviet-style socialist city. The warp and woof of socialist and capitalist urban life stand in marked contrast to one another. Observers of capitalist urban development are obsessed with the most overt manifestations of the market: ownership and transfer of private property, land values, the fees of real estate agents, appraisers and appraisal fees, taxes of various kinds, utility rates, consumption levels, media markets, and the like. Indeed, much of the English-language urban scholarship of the late 1980s neglected the political dimension of capitalist urban development, relegating the nuts and bolts of city politics to secondary status behind more impersonal forces of the urban political economy—such as economic restructuring, labor employment patterns, and demographic trends.[20]

Contemporary analysts of capitalist urban life—be they scholars or speculators—defer to the logic of international, national, and regional markets, understanding intuitively how their relentless "revaluation of uses" imposes order on the chaos of urban development. By examining market-oriented factors, commentators predict with swaggering confidence—although, to the consternation of many investors, certainly *not*

---

[20]This point is developed by Andrew E. G. Jonas in his review of over fifty works in urban theory appearing in English during the late 1980s and early 1990s: "A Place for Politics in Urban Theory: The Organization and Strategies of Urban Coalitions," *Urban Geography* 13, no. 3 (1993): 280–90.

always with accuracy—such monumental events as the cloning of Manhattan on New Jersey's Hudson shore, the movement of prime financial institutions from "The City" to London's Docklands, and the growth of Shibuya into one of Tokyo's most glitzy commercial centers.[21]

Observers of Soviet-style socialist urban development, by contrast, directed their energy to understanding the political and bureaucratic strategies employed within the state to achieve precise urban development goals.[22] Local Communist Party officials served as "prefects" for their regions, coordinating economic activity within their jurisdictions, smoothing complex bureaucratic rough edges, and mobilizing local resources behind development goals established, for the most part, elsewhere.[23] The national economic planning system under Gosplan, the state planning agency, similarly exerted considerable power over regional and local development.[24] As James Bater concluded in 1980, "To a large extent the degree to which the town-planning process in a particular city is successful or not depends upon the ability of the planner to gain political support, to effect bargains, to arrange compromises. In this regard his function is not so greatly different from his counterpart in the west. What does differentiate his role in the Soviet socialist system is the breadth of his mandate and the absence of competing, formal political forces which could be turned to for support."[25]

Confronting such a bureaucratic labyrinth, managers learned how to exert whatever political leverage they may have had through lobbying, personal connections, or hidden corruption to pursue urban development goals. The logic of city-building decisions was quite different from that of capitalist urban development. We can draw from the lore of contemporary Yaroslavl: visiting ministers and local potentates agreed, over vodka, about the placement of a university dormitory in the most inaccessible location possible; bridges were constructed on this site or that merely because of an offhand comment by a national leader; enor-

[21]The extent to which such predictions prove to be little more than promotional sensationalism is explored with some care by Gerald D. Suttles in *The Man-Made City: The Land-Use Confidence Game in Chicago* (Chicago: University of Chicago Press, 1990).

[22]See, for example, the essays in the classic collection by R. A. French and F. E. Ian Hamilton, eds., *The Socialist City: Spatial Structure and Urban Policy* (New York: John Wiley and Sons, 1979).

[23]Jerry Hough, *The Soviet Prefects: The Local Party Organs in Industrial Decision-Making* (Cambridge, Mass.: Harvard University Press, 1969).

[24]For further discussion of this point, see Judith Pallot and Denis J. B. Shaw, *Planning in the Soviet Union* (Athens: University of Georgia Press, 1981), pp. 34–51.

[25]James H. Bater, *The Soviet City: Ideal and Reality* (London: Edward Arnold, 1980), p. 55.

Figure 6. The "Yaroslavl White House," home to various regional and city councils and former headquarters building of the Yaroslavl Regional Committee of the Communist Party (Obkom). Photograph by Blair A. Ruble.

mous marble administration complexes were built simply because every other provincial center had its own "white house" (Figure 6).[26] Such locational decisions would have been quite different in form as well as in content under market conditions.

In Soviet-style socialist systems, political and bureaucratic power and resources were always more important than opportunity costs of alternatives and options. Cost constraints could not be easily or even accurately calculated. Competitive demand for inputs became unrestrained, since monetary shortfalls are much less binding in a socialist than in a capitalist environment. The resulting disequilibrium produced a sustained state of shortage.[27] Ultimately, the absence of cost constraints

[26]These examples are among the most popular and frequently repeated stories in Yaroslavl about the bureaucratic and political capriciousness of local urban planning decisions.

[27]The absence of real prices for resources also combined with the absence of popular review and control over industrial decision-making to contribute to the terrible environmental degradation of the entire Soviet landscape. This point is developed and explored in both Murray Feshbach and Alfred Friendly, Jr., *Ecocide in the USSR* (New York: Basic Books, 1992), and D. J. Peterson, *Troubled Lands: The Legacy of Soviet Environmental Destruction* (Boulder: Westview Press, 1993).

Figure 7. Nineteenth-century view of the Church of John the Baptist at Tolchkovo.

induced a voracious, near-insatiable demand that absorbed resources from both the producer and the consumer goods sectors.[28]

Without alternative use prices and with little fear of property taxes or popular dissent, demand for land became especially ravenous within the centrally planned socialist economy. Lack of access to senior state authorities frequently represented the only limit imposed on land use. Massive housing estates engulfed the landscape, since there was virtually no disincentive to consuming open space. Moreover, once built, enterprises had little impetus to move—even when the original locational decision had little to do with economic criteria.

THE FACTORY AND A CHURCH

The case of the Yaroslavl Church of John the Baptist at Tolchkovo illustrates this last point (Figure 7), since its sad fate had everything to do

[28]Janos Kornai, *Economics of Shortage* (Amsterdam and New York: North-Holland, 1980); Janos Kornai, " 'Hard' and 'Soft' Budget Constraints," *Acta Oeconomica* 25, nos. 3–4 (1980): 231–46.

with politics and virtually nothing to do with economics.[29] The church is a vibrant example of seventeenth-century Russian ecclesiastical architecture, which remains valued for its display of polychrome ceramic tiles.[30] These tiles—produced by local, Moscow-based, and foreign (probably Dutch) artisans—have been threatened by pollution emanating from a chemical-processing plant that literally embraces the church grounds. How did this happen?

A massive wave of church closings swept Russia following the Bolsheviks' 1929 law on churches. During the ensuing campaign, workers at the Pobeda Rabochikh (Workers' Victory) Paint and Lacquer Factory, just across the Kotorosl' River from central Yaroslavl, petitioned the local official newspaper *Severnyi rabochii (Northern Worker)* demanding that the metal roofs of the neighboring Church of John the Baptist be ripped down and turned over to industry to help alleviate the country's "metal and bronze famine."

The factory itself had been founded in the late nineteenth century by the Vakhromeev family, who had taken advantage of a local, several-centuries-long tradition of small workshops famous for enamel, lacquer, and ceramic craftwork. The Soviet government dramatically expanded this from a small-scale production plant to a monstrous paint and chemical factory. More space was needed, and the "workers soon demanded" that the municipal government "take down all of the bells from churches and turn them over to the task of industrializing the country."[31] Eventually, 1,534 paint and lacquer workers "voted" to expropriate the nearby church, and in 1936, the factory annexed the church grounds and buildings.[32] The church itself served as a cafeteria and, later, as a warehouse. Its spectacular frescoes were painted over, once again "at the behest of the workers" (Figure 8). Meanwhile, 3,000 workers in nearby Rostov-Veliki—perhaps the most important historic center of

---

[29]A brief history of the church and of the seventeenth-century Tolchkovo foreign settlement may be found in the Russian environmental newspaper *Spasenie* (Sergei Apal'kov, "Vsem tserkvam tserkov' . . . ," *Spasenie*, May 17–18, 1992, p. 7).

[30]For a discussion of the architectural significance of the Church of John the Baptist at Tolchkovo, see William Craft Brumfield, *A History of Russian Architecture* (New York: Cambridge University Press, 1993), pp. 159–61, and William Craft Brumfield, *Lost Russia: Photographing the Ruins of Russian Architecture* (Durham, N.C.: Duke University Press, forthcoming).

[31]Viacheslav Kozliakov, "Kogo strashil kolokol'nyi zvon?," *Iunost'* (Yaroslavl), May 20, 1989, p. 10.

[32]Apal'kov, "Vsem tserkvam tserkov'."

Figure 8. Frescoes in the Church of John the Baptist at Tolchkovo. Photograph by William C. Brumfield.

Russian bell music[33]—hauled down church towers as symbolic "votes for socialism."[34]

After being brought within the factory grounds for political purposes, the Church of John the Baptist suffered from severe pollution emanating from the surrounding chemical-processing equipment. Depending on whose version of this tale is believed, local authorities initiated efforts to renovate the church decades later either after the humiliating offer of an American businessman to purchase the church and move it brick by brick to the United States, or after a visit by Soviet Premier Nikita Khrushchev.

By the late 1980s, municipal leaders were encouraging the factory to move to a more remote location, away from the city center and its historic sites. Although unsuccessful in these attempts, city authorities were finally able to wrest control of the church complex itself away from the factory. In mid-1992, they transferred its buildings and immediately surrounding grounds to the Yaroslavl community of Old Believers.[35] Extreme air pollution continues to foil preservation efforts.

There should be little doubt that a private corporation or an entrepreneur could well have found it economically beneficial to construct a factory next to a historical monument. As urban critic Elizabeth Wilson warns, "Critical of the disasters of utopian planning, we are in danger of forgetting that the unplanned city still *is* planned, equally undemocratically, by big business and the multinational corporation."[36]

It is important to recognize that development decisions in a capitalist economy often involve at least some degree of greed, pure and simple. Once urban development expands and transportation links with downtown improve, a factory owner begins to consider relocating the plant

[33]V. Khrapchenko, "V gostiakh u 'Sysoia'," *Severnyi krai,* October 13, 1993, p. 2.
[34]Kozliakov, "Kogo strashil kolokol'nyi zvon?"
[35]Apal'kov, "Vsem tserkvam tserkov'." The Old Believers are a schismatic group that separated from the Russian Orthodox Church in a seventeenth-century revolt against rampant centralism in church and state during the reign of Tsar Aleksei Mikhailovich, the second ruler of the Romanov dynasty. The Orthodox Church and the tsarist government persecuted these Raskol'niki (schismatics) in various ways over the decades to follow—a pattern that intensified as a consequence of the belief among some Old Believers that Peter the Great was the Antichrist. Constantly at odds with state and ecclesiastic authority, Old Believer colonies were forced to fringe areas of the empire, especially in the far north. Their isolated communities fostered a spirit of pioneer self-reliance blended with a deep communal spirit. Yaroslavl became a center of efforts to preserve Old Believer culture during the 1970s and 1980s as a consequence of the activities on behalf of Old Believer communities by historians based at the local university.
[36]Elizabeth Wilson, *The Sphinx in the City: Urban Life, the Control of Disorder, and Women* (Berkeley: University of California Press, 1992), p. 152.

to less expensive land. Rising taxes based on land value and the cost of services encourage such a transfer, as does the profit that might be earned from resale of the land itself. The subsequent "higher use" might well prove more commodious to the historic structure previously engulfed by an industrial enterprise—at least, such is the theory of capitalist urban planning.

In Yaroslavl, the pattern has been rather different. No amount of prodding from city officials and preservation groups has induced the paint factory to move. The benefits of central location have not been offset by the economic incentives of rising land values. Consequently, the paint factory and the church remain locked in their illegitimate embrace despite the transfer of the sanctuary to the Old Believers (Figure 9).[37]

THE ROLE OF ECONOMICS IN CITY BUILDING

Economic forces certainly do not determine everything about urban development, even in an unbridled market. As Elizabeth Wilson reminds her readers, "Cities aren't villages; they aren't machines; they aren't telecommunication stations. They are spaces for face to face contact of amazing variety and richness."[38] The human contact that stands at the center of this urban experience, in turn, is determined by real live women and men who respond to an array of stimuli, including but not limited to economic trends.

Paul Kantor and Henry Savitch have argued in a somewhat similar vein that public and private economic and political structures are highly interdependent.[39] Advantage is derived, Kantor and Savitch conclude, by those local governments that are able to mobilize and legitimate both popular support and business interests simultaneously—regardless of variations in national political and economic structures around the world. Prominent Russian urbanist Vyacheslav Glazychev has contrib-

[37]Interview, Arkady Romanovich Bobovich, Chief Architect, Yaroslavl City Executive Committee, Yaroslavl, October 14, 1991.

[38]Elizabeth Wilson, *The Sphinx in the City: Urban Life, the Control of Disorder, and Women*, p. 158.

[39]Paul Kantor and H. V. Savitch, "Can Politicians Bargain with Business?: A Theoretical and Comparative Perspective on Urban Development," *Urban Affairs Quarterly*, December 1993; Paul Kantor and H. V. Savitch, "Urban Mobilization of Private Capital: A Cross-National Comparison," *Woodrow Wilson Center Comparative Urban Studies Occasional Paper Series, No. 3* (Washington, D.C.: Woodrow Wilson International Center for Scholars, 1993).

Figure 9. Church of John the Baptist at Tolchkovo bell tower, with Workers' Victory Paint and Lacquer Factory in the background. Photograph by William C. Brumfield.

uted to this debate by arguing that cultural attitudes in general combine with more specific notions of the city and urban life to precondition economic and political choice in city building.[40]

Theories of urban development that rely excessively on a single independent variable remain inadequate to the task of explaining city life. John Mollenkopf makes this point in his study of the rise and fall of New York Mayor Ed Koch. For Mollenkopf, space, place, and community all have importance in the exercise of power, since they constitute the building blocks of political dominance.[41] Mollenkopf was more explicit in a previous work, stating boldly, "By themselves, economic factors explain relatively little [about urban development]. They are necessarily mediated through, and influenced by, the political system."[42]

Fresh light is shed on these complex relationships by urban anthropologist Theodore Bestor, who observed that the more general forces at work in the give-and-take among cultural values, political decision-making, and economic behavior "often interact with one another in a manner much like the Japanese child's game of *jan-ken-pon:* rock crushes scissors, scissors cut paper, paper covers rock. Culture sustains institutions, institutions shape the economy, the economy recalibrates culture. . . . But it is clear—as in the child's game—that even if one viewpoint can temporarily demolish another, no one perspective can irreversibly clear all other contenders from the field. Economics, culture, and social institutions are inevitably conjoined."[43]

Just as it would be mistaken to overemphasize a single independent variable in studies of urban development, analysts should be cautioned against overstating the differences between economic systems. Capitalist and socialist city builders all "work their systems." Those involved in urban development respond to cultural norms and manipulate their environment differently under conditions of market-oriented and centrally administered systems. The devastation of the South Bronx neighborhood

[40]Vyacheslav Glazychev, "Social Change in Provincial Russian Towns" (seminar presentation at the Kennan Institute for Advanced Russian Studies, Washington, D.C., May 10, 1993).

[41]John Hall Mollenkopf, *A Phoenix in the Ashes: The Rise and Fall of the Koch Coalition in New York City Politics* (Princeton: Princeton University Press, 1992), pp. 34–43.

[42]John Hall Mollenkopf, *The Contested City* (Princeton: Princeton University Press, 1983), p. 8.

[43]Theodore C. Bestor, "Visible Hands: Auctions and Institutional Integration in the Tsukiji Wholesale Fish Market, Tokyo" (unpublished paper prepared for discussion by the Economic Sociology Workshop Group, Russell Sage Foundation, New York City, June 12, 1992), p. 2.

in New York City and the South Central neighborhood in Los Angeles may be explained only within the context of American attitudes toward race and class. Even so, the cityscape in both capitalist and socialist economic environments takes shape to a considerable extent—but never totally—in response to underlying economic conditions.

St. Petersburg planner-architect Boris Nikolashchenko captured the significance of the economic system for urban development by observing that the number of entryways along his city's main avenue—Nevskii prospekt—declined by two-thirds between 1914 and the 1980s, primarily as a consequence of the transition to a socialist economy.[44] The number of entryways has begun to increase as market forces have taken hold in the former Imperial capital, with smaller private concerns now replacing larger state monopolies. These changes have taken place despite considerable cultural continuity over the period. Similarly, an American visitor to Yaroslavl in 1911 called the city the "Hartford of Russia," with seventy-six churches and twenty millionaires.[45] The transition to Soviet-style socialism destroyed the city's capitalist social and political structure. Plants producing motors, tires, and synthetic rubber (allegedly the first such factory in the world) replaced textiles and trade as the city's motive economic force.[46] Russia's movement back toward a market system is producing yet another set of dominant institutions and groups, the pretensions of which will eventually determine the future form of provincial cities such as Yaroslavl.

TRANSITIONS TO MARKETS

Profit and property stand at the center of urban development decision-making in a market economy. One of the lessons of this study, then, will be that profits and property will grow in importance as Russian cities respond to a more market-oriented system of economic organization. "Money sings," as the young real estate mogul quoted at the outset of this study asserted. Cultural and planning institution managers, who

[44]Interview, Boris Vasil'evich Nikolashchenko, Chief, Scientific Research and Design Institute of the Master Plan for the Development of the City of St. Petersburg and Leningrad Region, St. Petersburg, September 13, 1991.

[45]Ruth Kedzie Wood, *Honeymooning in Russia* (New York: Dodd, Mead and Company, 1911), pp. 147–48.

[46]L. I. Kozlov and V. F. Marov, *Iaroslavl'. Putevoditel'-spravochnik* (Iaroslavl': Verkhne-volzhskoe knizhnoe izdatel'stvo, 1988), pp. 71–74; Andrei Treivish, "Tipichnyi krizis v tipichnom regione," *Vash vybor*, 1993, no. 1, pp. 12–13.

had never worried about turning a profit, now confront complex systems of accountability *(khozraschet)* that require earning revenues at least equal to expenditures.[47] State agencies have spawned cooperative ventures that actively seek profit.[48] Control of land and buildings has been called into question as conflicting Russian Federation and municipal laws, decrees, and administrative procedures obscure claims of ownership.[49] If property is to be privatized, by whom is it to be privatized? Which state agencies currently exercise control? Who decides what the process will be? Who is eligible to secure ownership of buildings? of land? Six years of Gorbachev-era perestroika followed by two more years of the Yeltsin-led first republic failed to provide definitive answers to such questions.

Russia's post-Soviet governments have only begun to grapple with the consequences of privatization. They have hardly even considered the impact of that process on urban life. A number of city leaders angrily confronted Russia's President Yeltsin in early 1992, pointing out correctly that his margin of victory in the June 1991 elections had been guaranteed by voters in medium-to-large urban centers.[50] Now was the time, they insisted in a tone all too familiar to American mayors, for Russia's cities to receive their due from the nation's political leaders in Moscow. Urban investment and predictability in urban policy, they argued, must become top priorities for the entire Russian government. Their pleas, again in a pattern well known to American urban leaders, failed to alter the course of federal policies.

Delays in initiating legislative and administrative reform during the first republic (August 1991–December 1993) intensified the mayhem of Russian municipal management and urban development. Central ministries vied with local officials for control of the economy, while the

---

[47]Interview, Elena Andreevna Ankudinova, Director, Architectural Division, Yaroslavl City Museum, Yaroslavl, June 25, 1990, and interview, Tatiana L'vovna Vasil'eva, Director, Yaroslavl Regional Administration for Preservation of Historic Monuments, Yaroslavl, June 25, 1990, and December 11, 1990.

[48]Interview, Iurii Ivanovich Verbitskii, Deputy, Yaroslavl City Soviet, and Chair, Commission on Culture of the Yaroslavl City Soviet, Yaroslavl, October 15, 1991.

[49]Interviews with: Iurii Mikhailovich Samoikin, Deputy, Moscow City Soviet, Moscow, July 2, 1990, and Trento, Italy, January 18–19, 1991; Viktor Mozolin, Section Chief, Institute of State and Law, USSR Academy of Sciences, Washington, D.C., October 31, 1990; Dmitrii Druzhinin, Deputy, Gagarin District Soviet (Moscow), Washington, D.C., April 23, 1991, and May 16, 1991; Nikita Maslennikov, Advisor on Land Use, St. Petersburg City Soviet, Washington, D.C., October 23, 1991; and Valerii Fadeev, Deputy, Moscow City Soviet, Washington, December 11, 1991.

[50]Discussion with Yaroslavl city official, April 28, 1992.

executive and legislative branches at all levels scrambled to advance mutually contradictory property and policy claims.[51]

URBAN ISSUES AND SYSTEMIC REFORM

In the pages that follow, this volume will examine housing privatization, historic preservation, and urban planning. On the housing front, Chapter 1 reviews the general Russian housing situation before the 1990s, setting forth the broad outlines of privatization efforts in 1991, 1992, and 1993. The discussion describes housing privatization programs in Moscow and St. Petersburg to provide a familiar context for an appraisal of Yaroslavl privatization initiatives.

Chapter 2 then examines the robust Yaroslavl privatization program, which successfully promoted the transfer of state apartments to private ownership throughout 1992. These efforts, which were supported by an activist political leadership, initially flourished. Mayor Volonchunas and city council leaders actively reached out to the community to generate enthusiasm for privatization schemes. The city council, for its part, established a commission to guarantee fairness in the privatization process. The rate of apartment privatization accelerated throughout 1992. The mortal political struggle in Moscow between a hard-line Russian Parliament and an embattled President Yeltsin brought a precipitous end to these encouraging developments. By early 1993, conflicting national laws and regulations confused Yaroslavl citizens and officials, paralyzing local housing privatization programs.

Chapter 3 highlights the often bitter disputes over historic preservation. The city and the region of Yaroslavl are rich in historic monuments. A vigorous local preservation movement emerged during the 1970s and 1980s in Yaroslavl, as elsewhere in the Soviet Union—this being one of the few legitimate areas for political activism. The local leaders of the "democratic" movement emerging from the 1989 and 1990 elections— in Yaroslavl as elsewhere in Russia—were frequently veterans either of the preservation crusade or of an active environmental movement.

The collapse of the Communist Party removed a shared opponent.

---

[51]For example, no fewer than four competitors—a private commodities exchange, a joint-stock company established by military officers, a local elected council, and the regional administration—grabbed title for a single fifty-four-hectare site that had been offered in May 1991 in the St. Petersburg suburb of Aleksandrovka for the construction of new single-family dwellings. Kaganova, "One-Family Housing Allotment."

The reality of post-Soviet Yaroslavl has proven too complex for simple approaches to preservation issues. Money now matters more than ever. Some local preservationists attempted to support their activities by earning profits on state-sponsored projects. Museum workers and church officials soon found themselves fighting for control of prominent buildings. Former Communist Party leaders hid behind their rights as property owners in conflicts with local authorities over the demolition of historic structures. A once united preservation movement frayed at the edges. Preservation programs became intertwined with the politics of urban space as concerned Yaroslavtsy sought to establish mechanisms for resolving the increasingly intense disputes over preservation philosophy, national identity, and property. In this fractious process, local courts may have managed to establish authoritative guidelines for managing the inevitable tensions between the rights of individual owners and the interests of communities intent on preserving their past.

Chapter 4 begins with the late-Soviet-era collapse of central planning authority, which freed hundreds of cities such as Yaroslavl from the straitjacket of overly centralized urban planning norms. The grasp of central planning authorities began to relax as early as 1987, when many communities across the country gained meaningful control over the physical planning process for the first time. In Yaroslavl, enthusiastic architects and planners persuaded city politicians to reevaluate their city's urban form. Working with Moscow contractors, city officials prepared competing projects for a new general plan. More conservative proposals foresaw continued urban development more or less along well-established lines, whereas more radical concepts encouraged a "re-ruralization" of the local population. Formal debate over these various proposals was set to begin in the city council just as President Yeltsin dismissed all local councils in October 1993. New municipal institutions are certain to revisit the issue sometime soon, once the institutional arrangements set forth in the 1993 constitution begin to function in reality.[52]

WHY DETAILS MATTER

Some readers may conclude that this volume becomes needlessly concerned with the minutiae of the policy process in a single provincial city.

---

[52]The Russian Federation Constitution approved by voters in December 1993 may be found in *Rossiiskaia gazeta*, November 10, 1993, pp. 3–6.

Yet, the precise impact of various reform and antireform initiatives is best seen precisely in such detail. By examining a limited set of issues in a single community, this volume seeks to add color and texture to discussions of reform in Russia. Dozens, probably hundreds, of similar snapshots will be required before commentators and practitioners can begin to come to terms with the impact of political, economic, and social change in such an enormous and diverse country as Russia.

Modest though they may be, the small interactions among local Yaroslavl citizens and politicians described here intimate some possible lessons about reform more generally in Russia. Local Yaroslavl political leaders have viewed their primary responsibility during the past half-decade as "cushioning the negative impact of reform."[53] These same politicians have simultaneously been remarkably creative in their approaches to making reform initiatives from above actually work in their community. Conservative by temperament, local officials—and citizens—seek to preserve as much as possible of familiar ways. They proceed quietly and cautiously, realizing all the while that fundamental change must take place if their community and their nation are to thrive politically and economically. Such tangled attitudes exist in a region and a city that have consistently supported first Gorbachev and then Yeltsin in various elections.[54] These are politicians and citizens who are open to reform and are resourceful in their response to reform initiatives but who simultaneously retain a deep provincial conservatism.

At a more general level, the actions reported in this study suggest that successful reform in Russia cannot come exclusively either from above or from below. Realization of reform programs requires many levels of Russian society to move more or less in the same direction. National reform politicians are wrong in viewing local elites as opposed to change, whereas Yaroslavl reform-minded politicians are equally misguided in their belief that Yaroslavl can somehow go it alone down a reform path. Yaroslavl reform initiatives in housing, historic preservation, and urban planning moved forward with dispatch when there were clear pro-

[53]Interview, Anatolii Ivanovich Lisitsyn, Chief of the Yaroslavl Regional Administration, and interview, Anatoli Fedorovich Guseev, Deputy Chief of Yaroslavl Regional Administration, Yaroslavl, April 15, 1993.

[54]Yaroslavl's relatively robust support for President Yeltsin may be seen, for example, in the comparatively strong endorsement of his policies in the April 25, 1993, referendum. A comprehensive and perceptive analysis of the results of that referendum may be found in Marie Mendras, "Les Trois Russies Analyse du referendum du 25 avril 1993," *Revue Française de Science Politique* 43, no. 6 (December 1993): 897–939.

reform signals from Moscow. This momentum dissipated as soon as mixed political signals began to emanate from Moscow. The reform impulse lost all power by mid-1993 as Russia's first post-Soviet government collapsed in the political infighting that eventually led to the storming of the Russian Parliament on October 3–4 of that year.

One of the lessons of this study will be that center and periphery must work in concert for new policies to be successfully implemented. The reform impulse in Yaroslavl is too strong to be stymied by antireform conservatives, yet too weak to move forward in the absence of clear direction from above. Any political structure that fails to bridge the economic and political gulf between central and regional elites will prevent progress.

1

Housing privatization

Privatization of housing is essential to ending the dependency of citizen on state, a hallmark of the Soviet regime. As Nathan Glazer has argued, empowerment begins when individual human beings exert control over their immediate environment.[1] Aside from giving a freer rein to those who want to reshape their lives, privatized housing carries with it a value that can be capitalized through rental, resale, and mortgaging. Title creates independent capital that can be drawn on by owners regardless of state intent. Ownership of one's abode engenders an autonomy—a freedom for individual action—that is a prerequisite for a functioning market.

Advocates of public housing in mature capitalist systems correctly point to the inability of private housing markets to meet all of the needs of the citizenry. "Privatization" as a slogan and as public policy can never be an adequate substitute for a comprehensive housing program. Mixed approaches to housing, as in so much of economic life at the end of the twentieth century, are required to optimize citizen well-being. The difficulty with Russian housing practices, however, is that the Soviet state never developed more than a rudimentary menu of approaches to providing the population with adequate housing.[2] The vast majority of Russians lived in public housing controlled either by their employers or by municipal agencies. With no claim to ownership, the typical Russian

---

[1]Nathan Glazer, "The Prince, the People, and the Architects," *American Scholar* 59 (Autumn 1990): 507–18.
[2]The Soviet housing period is reviewed in William Craft Brumfield and Blair A. Ruble, eds., *Russian Housing in the Modern Age: Design and Social History* (Cambridge: Cambridge University Press; Washington, D.C.: Woodrow Wilson Center Press, 1993).

at the end of the twentieth century has been nearly as dependent on the state for domicile as a serf was on his or her master at the beginning of the nineteenth century. Any serious effort in such a political and social environment to foster a more open political and economic system compels the creation of a private housing market.

The next two chapters will examine the evolution of urban housing privatization programs in post-Soviet Russia. This chapter will briefly review the evolution of housing policy following the death of Joseph Stalin in 1953. It will then rapidly evaluate the state of housing in Moscow, St. Petersburg, and Yaroslavl at the end of the Soviet era, before summarizing local privatization programs in Moscow and St. Petersburg.

The housing patterns in Russia's two largest cities have been chosen for comparison with Yaroslavl's housing pattern because both cities are more familiar to the outside world. The Moscow and St. Petersburg experiences provide interesting contrasts to housing configurations and policy initiatives in a Russian provincial city such as Yaroslavl. Closer to the centers of political power, both cities are home to advocates of reform and entrepreneurs well disposed to privatization of all economic resources including housing. International capital has driven local housing prices skyward, making ownership of title to one's apartment a considerable asset in its own right. Money sings more loudly in both metropolises than in provincial Yaroslavl.

The next chapter will examine Yaroslavl more directly, chronicling housing privatization there since the late 1980s. It will mark a shift in the discussion to a more Yaroslavl-centric focus. Comparisons with other Russian cities—most especially with Moscow and St. Petersburg—will occur throughout subsequent chapters as points of reference for readers unfamiliar with the standards, norms, traditions, and experiences of Yaroslavl residents.

HOUSING AND THE RISE OF KHRUSHCHEV

A lengthy and pressing agenda for change had accumulated during the last years before the death of Joseph Stalin despite a surface calm enforced by agencies of state security. Included among its items were an end to mass political terror, greater exposure to the outside world, increased flexibility in economic management, renewed investment in agriculture, expansion of consumer goods production, and an improved standard of living for the Soviet Union's poorest citizens. Together, these issues constituted a ready-made political program for any potential leader looking to depreciate the widespread image of hard-edged Kremlin politics. After some initial hesitation, Nikita Khrushchev moved to make this agenda his own, wielding it as one of several political clubs available for driving competitors off the national political stage.[3]

Housing lay at the heart of any attempt to add a populist sheen to Communist power.[4] Soviet housing conditions were shocking. The collectivization and rapid industrialization campaigns of the 1930s had forced tens of thousands of peasant families off the land into the already substandard urban housing left over from before World War I. The devastation of the Second World War, which had consumed vast expanses of the Soviet heartland, compounded an already appalling situation. The total destruction of frontline cities such as Kiev and Minsk and the extensive damage to other battered communities such as Leningrad ensured widespread dislocation and homelessness. A dearth of postwar construction did little to alleviate suffering. Perhaps a simple statistic best illustrates the common misery of that era: an average of 3.3 families lived in *each* Leningrad apartment in 1951—and Leningraders reputedly were much better housed than other Soviet citizens.[5]

Khrushchev moved into action on the housing front during mid-1955. He prompted the Communist Party and the Soviet architectural community to convene several conferences on housing, including a national gathering at the Moscow Architectural Institute and then another in the hallowed halls of the Kremlin.[6] By the end of the next year, three distinct bodies—the Twentieth Communist Party Congress, the Communist Party's Central Committee, and the all-union Council of Ministers—had issued proclamations announcing a housing program intended to provide each and every Soviet family with its own apartment over the course of the next three five-year plans.[7]

[3]Jerry F. Hough and Merle Fainsod, *How the Soviet Union Is Governed* (Cambridge, Mass.: Harvard University Press, 1979), pp. 192–210.

[4]This point was subsequently emphasized by Khrushchev himself in Nikita Khrushchev, *Khrushchev Remembers: The Last Testament*, trans. and ed. Strobe Talbott (Boston: Little, Brown, 1974), pp. 100–105.

[5]Denis J. B. Shaw, "Planning Leningrad," *Geographical Review* 68, no. 2 (April 1978): 189.

[6]See, for example, M. Kostandi, "Osobennosti planirovki malometrazhnykh kvartir," *Arkhitektura SSSR*, 1956, no. 6, pp. 10–14, and "Vsemerno uluchshat' tipovye proekty, povyshat' kachestvo massovogo zhilishchnogo stroitel'stva," *Arkhitektura SSSR*, 1956, no. 10, pp. 1–3.

[7]Discussions of these various decrees and resolutions may be found in the following:

The initial success of Khrushchev's housing program in providing families with new apartments eventually gave way to frustration over the quality, diversity, and flexibility of the new dwellings. An initial decade of success turned sour as the Soviet housing industry produced thousands of desperately needed apartments that few residents would find comfortable by the time of the Brezhnev "stagnation."

Citizen dissatisfaction resulted in part from the scale and achievements of the program. Unlike the situation in East European socialist states, single-family construction was not permitted in Russian cities with over one hundred thousand residents after 1961.[8] The absence of private construction restricted Russian urbanites to a monopolistic state housing market that never responded to shifting consumer preferences and needs.[9] The breach between the desired and the realized expanded as the program grew. Meanwhile, quality declined, with much of the housing stock that was constructed at the beginning of the housing drive deteriorating so quickly that it was becoming uninhabitable twenty years later.[10] The low quality of design and construction in much Soviet housing was very much a consequence of policies that treated habitation as just another "production problem" to be solved through "technological innovation."[11]

LATE SOVIET HOUSING IN MOSCOW

Three decades after the initiation of Khrushchev's massive housing program, geographic and class distinctions still mattered in the allocation

"Pravil'no, nauchno reshat' problemy tipizatsii zhilykh domov," *Arkhitektura SSSR,* 1956, no. 5, pp. 1–4; S. Khotchinskii, "Puti realizatsii stroitel'noi programmy," *Arkhitektura i stroitel'stva Moskvy,* 1957, no. 5, pp. 10–13; and S. Kibirev, "Arkhitektura i tipizatsiia massovogo zhilishchnogo stroitel'stva," *Arkhitektura SSSR,* 1968, no. 4, pp. 20–24. Also see Tsentral'nyi komitet KPSS, Sovet ministrov SSSR, "O razvitii zhilishchnogo stroitel'stva v SSSR (Postanovlenie 31 iiulia 1957 g.)," *Arkhitektura SSSR,* 1957, no. 9, pp. 1–6, and "Shire razvertyvat' zhilishchnoe stroitel'stvo," *Arkhitektura SSSR,* 1957, no. 10, pp. 29–30.

[8]This point is explored in Charles Hanson, Nadezhda Kosareva, and Raymond Struyk, "Housing Reform in the Russian Federation: A Review of Three Cities and Their Transition to a Market Economy," *Urban Institute International Activities Center Research Paper* (Washington, D.C.: Urban Institute, 1992 [March]), pp. 1–2.

[9]See further discussion in Bertrand Renaud, "The Housing System of the Former Soviet Union: Why the Soviets Need Housing Markets," *Housing Policy Debate* 3, no. 3, pp. 877–99.

[10]See, for example, the discussion in B. Kolotilkin, "Perspektivy ispol'zovaniia piatietazhnykh zhilykh zhdanii," *Arkhitektura SSSR,* 1979, no. 8, pp. 16–17, and G. D. Kubenko, "Komu ukroshchat' 'kovarnyi styk'?," *Leningradskaia panorama,* 1987, no. 7, pp. 39–40.

[11]This point is explored in greater detail in Ruble, "From *Khrushcheby* to *Korobki.*"

of living space. Discernible inequities remained in major cities such as Moscow at the end of the Soviet era. Total housing space and living space allotments for the average resident of the Russian capital's Leninskii district in 1989 (20.8 square meters and 13.2 square meters respectively) were nearly twice that of the average resident of the Solntsevskii district (11 square meters and 7.2 square meters). These differences had a significant impact on each resident's quality of life, given the diminutive space allocation of all but the best-housed Muscovites (the citywide averages at that time were 16.9 square meters for total housing allotment and 10.9 square meters for living space).[12] For comparison, it should be noted that average per capita housing allocations in 1990 were 52 square meters in Sweden and 51 square meters in the United States. By contrast, average allotments of 21 square meters in Bulgaria and 20.5 square meters in Poland were much closer to the Moscow norm.[13] Even the most fortunate Muscovites, then, had less space at their disposal than almost all their counterparts in Europe and North America—even in New York. Such comparisons become meaningful because these were precisely the points of reference to which most Muscovites themselves attached the greatest importance.

Ellen Hamilton, in an insightful examination of Moscow housing patterns at the end of the Soviet era, discerned significant residential social stratification in the capital. "The evidence presented," Hamilton wrote, "suggests that at the end of 1988 there existed in Moscow residential differentiation and that differences in housing quality were associated with variations in social status. Indeed, the system of housing allocation contributed to the development of what might be termed 'social areas.'"[14]

Moscow housing patterns were perhaps atypical in the sense that the capital's dwelling stock remained largely under municipal supervision. At the end of the Soviet period in 1990, 72 percent of all Moscow housing was controlled by municipal and district councils, and another 18 percent was in the purview of ministries and other state agencies.[15]

[12]Central Economic-Mathematical Institute, USSR Academy of Sciences, Socio-economic Data Base for Moscow, as reported in interviews at the institute on June 28, 1990.

[13]T. S. Kadibur, "Zhilishchnye usloviia naseleniia Sankt-Peterburga," in E. A. Poleshchuk and V. M. Makosii, eds., *Sankt-Peterburg v zerkale statistiki* (Sankt-Peterburg: Izdatel'stvo Sankt-Peterburgskogo universiteta ekonomiki i finansov, 1993), p. 13.

[14]Ellen Hamilton, "Social Areas under State Socialism: The Case of Moscow," in Susan Gross Solomon, ed., *Beyond Sovietology: Essays in Politics and History* (Armonk, N.Y.: M. E. Sharpe, 1993), pp. 192–225 (219).

[15]Hanson, Kosareva, and Struyk, "Housing Reform," pp. 1–2.

Public organizations—such as trade unions and cooperatives (roughly similar to the American apartment cooperative)—and individual owners held the balance. Comparable figures for the Russian Federation as a whole list 25 percent of housing in municipal hands, 42 percent under the ministries, and 26 percent under individual ownership, with the balance falling to public organizations and cooperative societies.

Distinctions in supervision and control reflected genuine disparities in the quality of housing. As Hamilton reminds her readers, little private housing was constructed after 1965, with the median year of construction for the capital's private housing stock being 1947. Housing cooperatives were nationalized in 1937 and were not permitted again until 1958, so that most cooperative housing buildings were constructed after that date. Ministerial housing was somewhat older (median year of construction being 1965) than municipal housing (with a median year of construction of 1969). Such variations reveal the consequences of oscillating housing policies under Stalin and Khrushchev.[16]

Finally, state housing in Moscow was of a higher quality than elsewhere in the country. Ministries and Communist Party organizations based in the capital were able to satisfy elite demand by ensuring higher-caliber—and a steadier supply of—construction materials by enforcing construction norms and by obtaining waivers from national limits on per capita living space. The pink-tinted brick apartment buildings of the Central Committee stood in stark contrast to the dingy, gray-brick structures going up elsewhere. The uncommon attention paid to the apartments of the *nomenklatura* (Soviet political and managerial elite) only accentuated social differentiation within Moscow itself.

THE ST. PETERSBURG HOUSING SCENE

Whatever the special factors molding Moscow housing patterns, St. Petersburg also exhibited significant social differentiation in terms of both the age and the size of housing allocations. The smallest per capita total housing space allotment in the city at the end of the Soviet era was 14.3 square meters in the Sestroretskii district—which, like Moscow's Solntsevskii district, had only recently been incorporated into the city limits.[17] The smallest total housing space allocations at that time in more traditionally urban districts were 15.3 square meters in the industrial

[16]Hamilton, "Social Areas under State Socialism," p. 208.
[17]Kadibur, "Zhilishchnye usloviia naseleniia Sankt-Peterburga," p. 14.

suburb of Kolpino and 16 square meters in the newer Krasnosel'skii district. Total housing allocations in the top-end districts of Oktiabr'skii (21.9 square meters) and Kuibyshevskii (21.0 square meters) were comparable to those in Moscow's Leninskii district. Interestingly, St. Petersburg's central Oktiabr'skii district also led the city in the percentage of communal apartments—in a pattern repeated in Yaroslavl.[18] But even though low-end per capita space allocations were somewhat larger than in Moscow, the configurations and floor plans of St. Petersburg apartments were frequently less felicitous. If, in Moscow, 81.9 percent of all households lived in their own apartments at the end of the Soviet era, only 68.4 percent of their counterparts in St. Petersburg were so fortunate. Of all St. Petersburgers, 23.8 percent lived in shared, multihousehold communal apartments (as opposed to 13.2 percent in Moscow).[19] These shared units were located primarily in older buildings downtown. As in Moscow, less than 1 percent of the St. Petersburg population in 1989 lived in individual private homes.[20]

The late Soviet-era housing stock in then-Leningrad had the additional peculiarity of being significantly differentiated by age. The combination of Stalinist inattention to housing construction and wartime destruction brought about a missing generation in the city's building stock. Whereas 71.1 percent of the city's 1989 housing stock had been constructed since 1961, fully 16.4 percent had been constructed before 1918 (with only 12.5 percent constructed in the intervening years—and almost all of that took place after World War II).[21] As a result, failure to obtain an apartment in one of the city's prefabricated high-rises (no treat in itself, as can be seen in Figure 10) often relegated the St. Petersburger to the decrepitude of undermaintained and overused prerevolutionary buildings downtown. This second form of inequitable distribution is considerably more important in St. Petersburg than in Moscow and Yaroslavl, where housing construction remained more robust throughout the Stalin era.

YAROSLAVL COMPARISONS

Turning to Yaroslavl, we find that the city's size, shape, and general physical form have influenced housing patterns as a number of districts

[18]Ibid.
[19]Ibid., p. 16.
[20]Ibid.
[21]Ibid., p. 21.

Figure 10. An example of Brezhnev-era housing projects in St. Petersburg. Photograph by Blair A. Ruble.

(raiony) have retained their own special face. These quite distinct dispositions, if not as sharply differentiated as Hamilton's "social areas" in Moscow, may nonetheless be discerned by a casual observer of Yaroslavl neighborhoods.

Dating from the eleventh century, the city's historic center follows an exceptional eighteenth-century street plan laid out roughly along the multiple intersections of two triangles focused on the now destroyed Cathedral of the Assumption (Figure 11).[22] Every second or third street forms an esplanade, usually ending on the embankments of one of the city's two rivers, the Volga and the Kotorosl' (Figure 12). A few junctions form squares, and others create parks. This street system, which was designed by Imperial planners under the reign of Catherine II, disturbed the Marquis de Custine when he visited Yaroslavl in 1839. Custine noted, "Notwithstanding its commercial importance, the city is

[22]The cathedral, which was severely damaged during the Bolshevik shelling of the city at the time of a White Guard rebellion in 1918, had been built in 1646. It was finally demolished in 1934 to make way for a gargantuan, five-hundred-unit Stalin-era apartment complex that, in turn, was never built. Viacheslav Kozliakov, "Vozvrashchaias' k napechatannomu. Novye demonstratsii ne nuzhny!," *Iunost'* (Yaroslavl), June 16, 1987, p. 3.

Figure 11. Late-nineteenth-century view of Demidov Lycée, with Cathedral of the Assumption in the background.

empty, dull, and silent. . . . Yaroslavl has its columns and its triumphal arches in imitation of Petersburg, all of which are in the worst taste, and contrast, in the oddest manner, with the style of the churches and stee-ples."[23] A century and a half later, these open spaces have been softened by the maturation of trees, and a perception of space that has been altered by the bombastic Soviet-era construction that now surrounds the historic city center. Central Yaroslavl today—which constitutes the core of the prestigious Kirovskii District—presents a strikingly congenial sense of place.

To the south across the Kotorosl' lies the Krasnoperekopskii District. Large settlements of old private wooden homes are interspersed with oil refineries and chemical and textile plants. Long the "wrong side of town," Krasnoperekopskii has been the least touched by the planners' dreams of the 1960s.

The third district, the Fruzhenskii, stands closer to the Volga—but still to the south of the Kotorosl'—and is the site of huge shipyards. Its private homes are more upscale, with the size of resident families running

[23]Astolphe Louis Leonor, Marquis de Custine, *Russia: Translated from the French of the Marquis de Custine* (New York: D. Appleton, 1854), p. 366.

Figure 12. Late-nineteenth-century view of Kazanskii Boulevard, Yaroslavl.

somewhat smaller than in the déclassé Krasnoperekopskii area (Figure 13). This second trans-Kotorosl' settlement is generally proletarian.

The fourth area, the Soviet-era factory belt of the Leninskii District, lies immediately to the north of the city center. Home to the city's famous textile plant, machine plant, and motor works, this area is the Soviet "rust belt" writ large. Its creation during the 1930s provided Yaroslavl with the sort of mid-century housing absent in St. Petersburg.

Yaroslavl's subcommunity across the Volga from the Leninskii District is the 1980s-era Zavolzhskii District (Figure 14). Connected to the city center by a single bridge, Zavolzhskii residents rely on a wholly deficient bus network. Residents must travel to the center for many basic provisions, since the district's service infrastructure has been built up more slowly than its new apartment complexes. The area is noteworthy for having one of the youngest populations in the city's subsettlements.

Finally, Zavolzhskii's twin and the city's sixth distinct precinct, the Dzerzhinskii District, incorporates many large enterprises that extend over its boundary with the Leninskii District, together with the Bragino area to the north. "Bragino" is the popular appellation for the "Northern Settlement Zone." This nickname is derived from *braga*, a traditional home-brewed and illicitly produced beer with which this area

Figure 13. Soviet-era private homes in the Fruzhenskii District of Yaroslavl. Photograph by Blair A. Ruble.

was long associated. Bragino now includes much of the city's newest public housing and has become home to a large part of the city's white-collar work force.

PROVINCIAL EGALITARIANISM

Local housing data from 1989 reveal that housing was markedly more equitably distributed in Yaroslavl than in Moscow.[24] Moreover, the city's standards for unit size and ownership were closer to national Russian norms.

Yaroslavl residents at the end of the Soviet era inhabited a variety of state apartments and privately owned homes. The latter, which constituted about one-fifth of the city's housing stock, provided a quality of life that was nowhere near as homey as might appear at first glance. Most private homes were at least three decades old and had little insu-

---

[24]These observations about the nature of the Yaroslavl housing stock are based on discussions with representatives of the Statistical Administration of the Yaroslavl Regional Executive Committee on June 19, 1990.

Figure 14. A new housing district in the Zavolzhskii District of Yaroslavl. Photograph by Blair A. Ruble.

lation, and many also lacked running water. State apartments, in turn, were either municipal property or under the control of individual factories, such as the giant Avtodizel' Motor Works. A small number of higher-quality cooperative apartments were built throughout the Brezhnev era in Yaroslavl, as elsewhere (Figure 15). This semiprivate sector remained the preferred housing of many midlevel political and intellectual figures, thereby ensuring that market forces were never totally absent in pre-Gorbachevian housing patterns.

Quantitative and qualitative differences in Yaroslavl housing allotments in 1989 were considerably less striking than in Moscow, more closely approximating the pattern in St. Petersburg.[25] Only a very few of the *nomenklatura*-quality buildings that dominate central Moscow were constructed in this provincial capital. As in St. Petersburg, the largest allocations—of 16.3 square meters of total housing and 10.4 square meters of living space—were found in the city's historic central area—

[25]Goskomstat RSFSR, Iaroslavskii gorodskoi otdel statistiki, *statisticheskii biulleten'. Dannye o zhilishchnom fonde goroda Iaroslavlia za 1989 god* (Iaroslavl': Goskomstat RSFSR, Iaroslavskii otdel, February 1990).

Figure 15. A 1980s cooperative apartment building in Yaroslavl. Photograph by Blair A. Ruble.

the Kirovskii District—which also contained the community's highest concentration of communal apartments (approximately one-quarter of all Kirovskii district residents shared facilities in *kommunalki*). The Krasnoperekopskii District provided the most modest space allocations in the city, with average allotments in 1989 of total housing space at 15.6 square meters and living space at 9.5 square meters. Not only were state allocations in the Krasnoperekopskii District somewhat more meager than the city norm, but a high percentage of district residents inhabited privately owned wooden cottages. The surprising result is that the data for the Krasnoperekopskii district were not farther removed from the Yaroslavl-wide norm of 15.9 square meters for total housing allotments and 9.9 square meters for living space allotments.

LEGISLATING A PRIVATE HOUSING MARKET

Housing patterns in post-Soviet Yaroslavl are now being determined by the market. The very first guidelines for the privatization of housing were announced by the USSR Council of Ministers in December 1988 and were expanded by a joint decree of the Council of Ministers and the All-Union Central Council of Trade Unions four months later.[26] By May 1990, privatization proposals stood at the center of Mikhail Gorbachev's presidential decree on housing issues.[27] The Russian Federation government launched its own, more aggressive privatization initiatives after passage of a July 1991 law on housing privatization.[28]

The pivotal July 1991 Russian Federation law established the principle that resident families were eligible to receive, free of charge, no less than 9 square meters per family plus 18 square meters per family member.[29] Municipalities were required to determine the precise means for title transfer, including compensation requirements for those families occupying less space than the minimal norm and payment requirements for those inhabiting a larger area. The law exempted or limited enterprise housing and housing controlled by social organizations, as well as collective and state farm housing, from privatization regulations.

The importance of housing concerns in the overall reform process was evident in the Declaration of Human Rights and Freedoms adopted by the Soviet Congress of People's Deputies in the wake of the failed August 1991 putsch.[30] That act established far-reaching housing rights, including the right of citizens "to move freely inside the country, choose residence and location" (article 21), to "enjoy property rights" (article 24), and "to state support in receiving and permanently utilizing an apartment with basic amenities" (article 27). These rights were reflected in subsequent policies of the Russian Federation following the collapse of the Soviet Union itself. An even more aggressive privatization program approved by the Russian cabinet at the end of 1991 established guidelines for the privatization of agricultural land.[31]

[26]K. A. Glukhov, *Privatizatsiia zhil'ia (kommentarii k zakonodatel'stvu)* (Moscow: Iuridicheskaia firma "Paritet," MGU im. M. V. Lomonosova, 1991), part 1, pp. 3–5.

[27]Ibid., p. 3.

[28]"Zakon RSFSR o privatizatsii zhilishchnogo fonda v RSFSR ot 4 iiulia 1991 g." and "Postanovlenie Verkhovnogo soveta RSFSR o vvedenii v deistvie zakona RSFSR o privatizatsii zhilishchnogo fonda v RSFSR," in ibid., part 2, pp. 3–15. The importance of this act is discussed in Lynn D. Nelson, Lilia V. Babaeva, and Rufat O. Babaev, "Perspectives on Entrepreneurship and Privatization in Russia: Policy and Public Opinion," *Slavic Review* 51, no. 2 (Summer 1992), pp. 270–86 (275–76), as well as in O. Z. Kaganova, "Creating an Urban Real Estate Market in Russia," *Real Estate Issues* 18, no. 1 (Spring/Summer 1993): 45–48.

[29]Glukhov, *Privatizatsiia zhil'ia*, part 1, pp. 5–17.

[30]"Text of Rights Adopted by the Soviet Congress," *New York Times*, September 7, 1991, p. 5.

[31]Keith Bush, "Russian Privatization Program Approved," *RFE/RL Daily Report*, no. 243 (December 27, 1991): 2; Keith Bush, "Land Privatization Decree," *RFE/RL Daily Re-*

Privatization of land remained completely muddled throughout the first republic, with the well-known infighting between conservative parliamentarians and reform-minded executive branch officials blocking the enactment of national legislation that would set forth concise and enforceable property rights for land. By the end of 1992, Russian citizens had the right to buy and sell private plots of land, provided that the land was not used for commercial purposes.[32] Ten million hectares (24.7 million acres) had been acquired by 16 million urban families during the year and by 4 million rural families for gardening or for constructing private housing.[33] There also were, by the end of 1992, 173,000 private commercial farmers, 2,300 agricultural cooperatives, and 19,000 livestock collectives, despite the bureaucratic difficulties in the purchase of land. Russians immediately began to position themselves to take advantage of legislative proposals that were thought to establish the right to purchase urban land as well.[34]

A new "Fundamentals of Land Legislation," approved by the Russian Federation Parliament on July 21, 1993, finally established the juridical basis for a land market.[35] Implementation, however, immediately fell prey to the intensifying constitutional crisis that ultimately resulted in the ill-fated parliamentary insurrection two months later. According to this law, private individuals, municipalities, and the state could own land. Foreign citizens or organizations would be able to lease land only for temporary use and could not retain title of ownership.[36] The Fed-

port, no. 244 (December 30, 1991): 2; Keith Bush, "Enterprise Privatization Decree," *RFE/RL Daily Report,* no. 244 (December 30, 1991): 2; Keith Bush, "Privatization in Russia," *RFE/RL Daily Report,* no. 1 (January 2, 1992): 2.

[32]This right was reconfirmed in February 1992 at the regional level by the regional soviet's mini-council (Malyi sovet Iaroslavskogo oblastnogo soveta narodnykh deputatov, "Reshenie No. 234 o prodazhe zemel'nykh uchastkov pri privatizatsii imushchestva v oblasti" [February 26, 1992]). Also see discussion in Kaganova, "Creating an Urban Real Estate Market in Russia."

[33]Sheila Marnie, "Land Reform in Russia," *RFE/RL Daily Report,* no. 1 (January 4, 1993): 1.

[34]Interview, Bobovich, October 14, 1991; Philip Hanson, "Housing Problems," *RFE/RL Daily Report,* no. 129, (July 10, 1991): 7; N. A. Savinova and T. V. Iurepina, eds., *Privatizatsiia. Polnyi paket dokumentov* (Moscow: Rossiiskoe pravo, 1992). An English translation of the law passed by the Russian Federation Parliament on August 3, 1991, concerning privatization of enterprises was published in June 1992 by *Moscow Business Week,* "a free newspaper for people with choices" ("Law of the RSFSR on Privatization of State and Municipal Enterprises," *Moscow Business Week,* no. 12 [June 4, 1992]: 7–10). Also see the discussion in Kaganova, "Creating an Urban Real Estate Market in Russia."

[35]Sheila Marnie, "Russian Parliament Approves Land Legislation," *RFE/RL Daily Report,* no. 138 (July 22, 1993): 2.

[36]This was a departure from proposals put forward by the previous government of Yegor Gaidar, who, in June 1992, reported that the Federation government would propose that

eration's Committee for Land Resources and Land Tenure and its subordinate agencies had secured authority at last over the use and protection of land throughout the Federation. Additional enabling legislation governing the sale and mortgaging of land was required to complete the legal framework for real estate transactions.

Further legal mechanisms governing landownership would have to await the emergence of a new Russian state system following the collapse of the first republic in early October 1993. Yeltsin and Boris Nemtsov, the chief of the Nizhnii Novgorod Regional Administration, announced a pilot privatization program for land on October 27, 1993.[37] The Yeltsin Constitution, adopted on December 12, 1993, included the right to private property among those rights to be guaranteed to every citizen of the Russian Federation.[38] Constitutional declarations and local experiments presumably will be followed during the second republic by the elaboration of national mechanisms for finally implementing land-reform initiatives.

LOCAL RESPONSES TO NATIONAL POLICIES

As notable as these national decrees, declarations, and laws may have been in their own right, they had mixed reviews in Yaroslavl and in many other communities. A number of technical issues were left to local discretion, including the transfer of title, the eligibility of collective farm and state enterprise housing for privatization, the rights of family members to a share of privatized title, and payment of required capital repairs. Lingering uncertainties—if left unresolved by the post-1993 Russian government—undoubtedly will guarantee the livelihood of a new class of real estate and housing lawyers for some time to come.[39] Local action by individual municipalities provides intriguing evidence of the difficulties encountered by those who foresaw widespread privatized housing in Russia's future.

Initially, privatization programs progressed further in Moscow than

---

foreigners be allowed to buy nonagricultural land (Fred Hiatt, "Yeltsin to Let Foreigners Buy Russian Land," *Washington Post,* June 13, 1992, p. A15). This proposal failed to sustain political support after Gaidar left office later that year.

[37] Fred Hiatt, "Yeltsin Launches Plan to Spur Private Land Ownership," *Washington Post,* October 27, 1993, p. A27.

[38] Celestine Bohlen, "Yeltsin Promotes a Charter That Is Very Much His," *New York Times,* November 10, 1993, p. A18.

[39] Glukhov, *Privatizatsiia zhil'ia,* part 1, pp. 23–30.

elsewhere before collapsing altogether at the end of 1991 in the wake of bitter political battles between Mayor Gavriil Popov and the Moscow City Council.[40] The Moscow City Council authorized the sale of apartments to current residents in December 1990. Trial auctions and sales began the following spring.[41] Municipal authorities then prepared guidelines for the widespread sale of state apartments to residents by the autumn of 1991.[42] According to a plan proposed by Mayor Popov, each Moscow family was to be entitled, free of charge, to 12 square meters of housing space plus an additional 18 square meters for each family member (these norms were the same as those set in St. Petersburg but were slightly more generous than those contained in the Russian Federation legislation of July 1991).[43] Residents were to receive coupons to purchase this amount of living space. Those living in apartments that were smaller than this norm would receive coupons totaling the larger space allocation free of charge. Those with apartments that already contained more space than the projected norm would be able to purchase additional coupons at a proposed rate of R203.40 per additional square meter of general living space (U.S. $5 at the time). Future buyers would then have been able to purchase or sell living space and housing coupons through the city's housing exchange. The Moscow City Council anticipated organizing financial-assistance programs for those who wanted to purchase apartments, at an interest rate of 20 percent over a five-year term.

Political disputes between Mayor Popov and the Moscow City Council escalated throughout the autumn of 1991.[44] Popov declared that title for all Moscow apartments would be given to residents free of charge regardless of the apartment size. The city council countered that such an

[40] A chronicle of competing decrees, laws, and regulations issued before November 1991 by the Moscow City Council, the mayor's office, and various district or ward *(raion)* bodies is provided in Glukhov, *Privatizatsiia zhil'ia*, part 1, pp. 17–23.

[41] Dmitrii Volkov, "Moszhiluchet budet prodavat' kvartiry s auktsiona," *Kommersant*, February 18–25, 1991, p. 4; Elena Berezneva, "Vse khotiat delit'. Kto budet stroit'?," *Kommersant*, April 19, 1991, p. 1; Natalia Davydova, "Vse blizhe, i blizhe, i blizhe," *Moskovskie novosti*, no. 16 (April 21, 1991): 4; Dmitrii Skladchikov, "Pervyi auktsion kvartir v Moskve: million za rublevki," *Kommersant*, April 22–29, 1991, p. 5.

[42] Keith Bush, "Popov's Plans for Moscow," *RFE/RL Daily Report*, no. 179 (September 19, 1991): 1; Moskovskii gorodskoi sovet narodnykh deputatov, "Proekt: Osnovnye dokumenty po privatizatsii Moskovskogo gorodskogo zhilishchnogo fonda" (Moscow, 1991).

[43] Vladimir Gel'man and Mary McAuley, "The Politics of City Government: Leningrad/St. Petersburg," in Jeffrey W. Hahn and Theodore Friedgut, eds., *Local Power and Post-Soviet Politics* (Armonk, N.Y.: M. E. Sharpe, 1994), pp. 15–42: 35.

[44] Interview, Nikolai Zlobin, Professor, Moscow State University, Washington, D.C., January 4, 1992.

arrangement would unjustly reward formerly well-connected families with larger apartments. The council reversed the Popov proposal, raising the price for all supplemental living space over the 12/18 square meter formula to approximately R900. Residents lined up at local housing offices to purchase title to their apartment only to discover that the mayor or city council had reversed the other's most recent policy. Total chaos reigned in the Moscow housing market by the end of the year. Renewed guidelines issued in early 1992 by the mayor's office, with the backing of Russian Federation President Yeltsin, eventually brought about an initial wave of apartment privatization, but great resistance remained in many government agencies and among a population fearful of rising costs in a time of inflation.[45]

Moscow officials responsible for administering this program had expressed incredulity over proclamations that housing would be given away for "free" well before squabbling erupted between the mayor and the city council. Those inhabiting space allotments in excess of the proposed norm were going to be forced to pay rather large supplemental fees merely to remain in their own apartments. Maintenance charges, the officials continued, were likely to be considerably higher than previous Soviet-era subsidized rental rates. Finally, no organizational structures or procedures had been put into place before the promulgation of the privatization plan. As a result, privatization was viewed, in the words of one district soviet official in Moscow, as "yet another painful illusion."[46]

The privatization of Moscow housing eventually proceeded more smoothly later on, but hardly without controversy.[47] Conflict between the city council and the mayor's office abated as relations between the executive and the legislature became more predictable after Mayor Popov's resignation in mid-1992. Moscow construction agencies squirreled away funds that were intended for financing the privatization of existing housing and have drawn on them to construct new rental housing at market prices (usually at 35 percent above the cost of construction). A significant number of units had been privatized by the end of 1992—

[45]Louis Uchitelle, "Now All Moscow Apartments Have a View," *New York Times,* February 28, 1992, p. A10.

[46]Interview, Vladimir Ivanovich Polunin, Chair, Kiev District Council (Moscow), Moscow, October 17, 1991.

[47]This account is based on a report of then Moscow vice-mayor Iurii Luzhkov to the Moscow City Soviet in May 1992 (Ivan Rodin, "Vitsemer nedovolen birzhei nedvizhimosti," *Nezavisimaia gazeta,* May 16, 1992, p. 6).

more than 340,000 by November of that year.[48] These gains—which appear to have been prompted in part by the increasing demand from a rapidly growing foreign community—occurred despite the fact that much of the floor space that was being made available to residents free of charge ended up in the hands of bureaucrats in charge of the privatization programs. Moreover, only 102 of 449 ministries and organizations maintaining housing for their Moscow employees had initiated privatization programs during 1993—the remaining 347 resisted programs to turn their apartments over to residents.

The growing presence of foreigners in the Russian capital quickly drove housing prices upward throughout 1993. With predictable rules of the privatization game more or less in place (although not always established in law), Muscovites moved with accelerating speed to privatize their apartments either to protect their homes or to turn a quick profit. Money meant more in Moscow than at any other time since the Bolsheviks had come to power.

In St. Petersburg, movement toward privatization was similarly stymied by conflicts, among the various state agencies, about the allocation of authority over specific buildings.[49] Featured in the 1989 and 1990 campaigns of many reform-oriented local politicians, privatization was greeted by an early burst of enthusiasm, which soon wavered in the face of the imposing complications caused by the age of the city housing stock, the large number of communal apartments (*kommunalki*) in central districts, and the shortage of city funds to maintain more modern buildings.[50] By late 1991, a number of vicious battles among soviets and executive committees, the city, the region (oblast), and districts had been resolved by having smaller structures assigned to the oversight of districts and larger buildings listed under the jurisdiction of the city of St. Petersburg itself.[51]

Nani Kulish Boyce, drawing on stories appearing in the Russian business weekly *Kommersant,* reported that "only eight private apartments in the city [St. Petersburg] and four homes in the countryside" had been

---

[48]Sheila Marnie, "Privatization of Housing," *RFE/RL Daily Report,* no. 218 (November 11, 1992): 2.

[49]See, for example, the discussion in Kaganova, "One-Family Housing Allotment"; Erlanger, "In St. Petersburg, a Fight over Power and Property"; and Nani Kulish Boyce, "Russia on the Way to a Housing Market: A Case Study of St. Petersburg," *Environment and Planning Annual* (Great Britain) 25 (1993): 975–86.

[50]Gel'man and McAuley, "The Politics of City Government," pp. 34–36.

[51]Interview, Olga Kaganova and Nikita Maslennikov, Advisors on Land Use, St. Petersburg City Soviet, Washington, D.C., October 22, 1991.

offered at auction between November 1991 and January 1992.[52] The prices—ranging from R1.5 million to R2.4 million ($15,000 and $24,000, respectively, at that time) for homes and R170,000 and R450,000 ($1,700 and $4,500) for the apartments—reflect great price fluctuation in a limited market in which demand exceeds supply.

Limited housing sales aside, quarrels over the allocation of decision authority between executive and legislative agencies continued. Large-scale privatization of existing state housing eventually began only after local St. Petersburg agencies had settled their own disputes over the disposition of existing housing. As elsewhere, the pace of privatization accelerated during 1992 as citizen and city official alike gradually came to understand the complex rules governing the transfer of title to apartment residents. By mid-year, some four hundred thousand St. Petersburg families had successfully privatized or had initiated the privatization process for their apartments.[53] At year-end, residents had privatized approximately 14 percent of the state housing stock in the city.[54] As in Moscow, prices rose and the pace of privatization quickened throughout 1993, especially as a nascent foreign community began to feel more secure. However, as will become apparent in an examination of housing privatization in Yaroslavl, it was at about this time that the Russian Federation once again changed the rules of the privatization game.

STRUCTURAL IMPEDIMENTS TO PRIVATIZATION

Important as the rules of the privatization process have been in establishing the scale and pace of various programs, the experience in a variety of Russian towns and cities also reveals very real structural constraints to the transfer of title to apartment residents. The absence of a developed service sector, for example, left new home owners at the mercy of the same inadequate municipal agencies as before. Meanwhile, inequitable housing patterns necessarily created a somewhat capricious distribution of winners and losers in the privatization game. The failure to mold a comprehensive housing policy around privatization goals similarly confounded local administrators even when they concluded that

---

[52]Nani Kulish Boyce, "Housing in St. Petersburg, Russia: From a Centrally-Planned System to the Western-Market Orientation" (unpublished manuscript prepared at the Urban Transportation Center, University of Illinois at Chicago, May 8, 1992), p. 13.

[53]Kaganova, "Creating an Urban Real Estate Market in Russia," p. 46.

[54]Gel'man and McAuley, "The Politics of City Government," p. 36.

the time had come to act.[55] Virtually no financial institutions existed to assist individual buyers and owners with credit and other forms of monetary support. Construction supplies remained limited in design and in availability. The basic legal, administrative, and private-sector supports required to operate a private housing market had yet to take shape as the first republic came to an end in late 1993.[56]

The very form of Soviet housing construction over the past several decades contributed its own impediments to the privatization program. State construction trusts built apartments that were uniquely unsuited to private ownership. The difficulty is not only that these are almost exclusively small, individual units within behemoth apartment blocks but also, more profoundly, that all municipal housing was planned and constructed with other goals in mind.

First, Khrushchev's industrialized construction program was intended to provide an apartment for each Soviet family rather than to create a mobile housing market. Consequently, variation in design standards and floor plans remained unduly limited, consumer choice was virtually nonexistent, and families were forced to make do with what was available.[57] Few Russians were able to shape their domestic environment during the Soviet era.

Second, the breakdown of civil authority that accompanied Gorbachevian perestroika fostered a more general decline in public dignity and decorum. Most North Americans and Europeans would describe the dank lobbies of even the best contemporary Russian apartment buildings as slumlike. Russians frequently had a similar response.

The nature of public space is a direct consequence of the tyranny of post-Khrushchevian industrialized construction technologies. Early in the development of these methods, engineers concluded that the design of public spaces would be too burdensome and wasteful a task. Entryways and corridors were kept to a minimum so as not to complicate the prefabricated design and the block-section construction methods so adored by engineers. Although bourgeois pretensions are easily mocked, it is clear that the ennobling experience born of certain middle-class

---

[55]These points were emphasized in interview, Nadezhda Leonidovna Ershova, Head of the Housing Privatization Office of Yaroslavl City, Yaroslavl, April 16, 1993, and September 8, 1993.

[56]For additional discussion of these concerns, see Aleksandr Vysokovskii, "Will Domesticity Return?," in Brumfield and Ruble, *Russian Housing in the Modern Age,* pp. 271–308.

[57]I explore these themes in greater detail in "From *Khrushcheby* to *Korobki.*"

affectations in Western apartments built over the past century is sorely absent from current Russian housing.[58] Today's shabby lobbies and hallways devalue Russian apartments precisely at the moment when policymakers have begun to introduce market mechanisms into the housing sector.

Third, the inflexibility of the Soviet construction industry prevented the birth of creative responses to deficiencies readily acknowledged by both architects and the general public alike. Builders and their suppliers had lost the capacity to utilize alternative modes of construction. Russian housing authorities had become trapped in a straitjacket imposed by technological imperatives that remained unchecked by the pluralism of market demands.

Nathan Glazer has observed that designers in the modern era have failed to explore what it is that people find attractive in their homes. Apartment towers "show no opportunity for change. How could they, since their residents have so little power over their environment?"[59] Wolfgang Braunfels expressed the same critical perspective in slightly different terms when he noted, "The freedom to participate in the design of one's own urban living environment has been a prerequisite for the success of towns. One cannot plan for strangers."[60] The Western alienation from residence—so decried by Glazer and Braunfels—was magnified in the Soviet Union, where all planning was done for strangers. It was against this backdrop that Yaroslavl administrators were forced to fashion their own local policies to meet national goals for housing privatization.

---

[58]It is true, of course, that a sense of enrichment is regrettably absent from many contemporary apartment houses in the capitalist world as well. Still, grand public spaces have been frequently added to make middle-class and elite apartment dwellings in Europe and North America appear to be more houselike. See, for example, the discussions in Françoise Loyer, *Paris Nineteenth Century: Architecture and Urbanism*, trans. Charles Lyon Clark (New York: Abbeville Press, 1988), pp. 231–71; James M. Goode, *Best Addresses: A Century of Washington's Distinguished Apartment Houses* (Washington, D.C.: Smithsonian Institution Press, 1988), pp. 528–41; Thomas E. Norton and Jerry E. Petterson, *Living It Up: A Guide to the Named Apartment Houses of New York* (New York: Atheneum, 1984), pp. 2–25; E. C. Cromley, *Alone Together: A History of New York's Early Apartments* (Ithaca, N.Y.: Cornell University Press, 1990), pp. 134–48; and Elizabeth Hawes, *New York, New York: How the Apartment House Transformed the Life of the City (1869–1930)* (New York: Alfred A. Knopf, 1993).

[59]Glazer, "The Prince, the People, and the Architects," pp. 505–18 (515).

[60]Wolfgang Braunfels, *Urban Design in Western Europe: Regime and Architecture, 900–1900*, trans. Kenneth J. Northcott (Chicago: University of Chicago Press, 1988), p. 368.

2

Privatization comes to Yaroslavl

The same pressures and anxieties that pushed local officials in Moscow and St. Petersburg to endorse the mass privatization of state housing were at work in Yaroslavl. Reformers in President Yeltsin's government spoke of the need to create a middle class of property owners who would support the rapid transition to a market economy. Budget officials estimated the costs of maintaining massive apartment complexes and calculated the expanding drain on municipal resources. Local plant managers and trade union officials spoke out against turning over factory housing to residents, on the grounds that privatization represented yet another stage in state expropriation of property (e.g., the property of enterprises and trade unions).

In Yaroslavl, housing privatization retained a coherence and clarity that was missing in many of Russia's largest cities. Much smaller and less diverse than Moscow and St. Petersburg, Yaroslavl moved more slowly with privatization programs. In the end, however, the story of housing privatization in Yaroslavl remained essentially the same as elsewhere in Russia.

HOUSING PRIVATIZATION BEGINS

Yaroslavl officials concerned with the city's development initially tackled the issue of land valuation before turning to housing privatization. Calculating that land values would inevitably determine settlement patterns, the Yaroslavl City Council adopted resolutions in June 1991 instructing city planning officials to bring local land-use practices into conformity with new land legislation that had just passed the Russian Federation

51

Parliament.[1] The Architectural and Planning Administration of the Yaroslavl City Executive Committee undertook surveys in conjunction with
a Moscow-based team of consultants in order to calculate initial land
values in twelve zones within the city.[2] These rates varied from a proposed land rent of R55,000 (U.S. $430 at that time) per hectare in north-
ern fringe areas of the Zavolzhskii District to R92,000 ($700) per
hectare downtown. Anticipating a rush to claim urban land, the Yaroslavl City Council's mini-council established a special commission in
April 1992 to adjudicate disputed land claims.[3] The larger city council
reserved the right to serve as tribunal of last resort. As will become
apparent later in this chapter, the failure of national institutions to develop urban land policy eventually brought local initiatives such as these
to a halt.

City officials next reviewed procedures governing housing privatization in late 1991.[4] Claiming authority over all state housing—even that
built by individual state enterprises for their own employees—the city
council enacted its own privatization initiatives in early 1992.[5] Apartments smaller than or equal in size to established norms were to be
transferred to private ownership free of charge.[6] Special provisions were
designed to expedite the transfer of title to the families of military officers and survivors of the Chernobyl nuclear accident.[7]

Yaroslavl standards were moderately more generous than those of the
Russian Federation law: 10 square meters per family plus an additional

[1]Iaroslavskii gorodskoi sovet narodnykh deputatov, Shestaia sessiia dvadtsat' pervogo sozyva, "Reshenie ot 25.06.91 o merakh po obespecheniiu ekonomiko-pravogo regulirovaniia pol'zovaniia zemel' n' ymi resursami g. Iaroslavlia" (June 25, 1991).
[2]Interview, Bobovich, October 14, 1991, and Iaroslavskii gorodskoi ispolnitelnyi komitet,
"Iaroslavl'. Skhema goroda: ekonomicheskoe zonirovanie territorii" (1991).
[3]Malyi sovet Iaroslavskogo gorodskogo soveta narodnykh deputatov, "Reshenie No. 72
Malogo soveta i Postanovlenie Mera goroda No. 384 o rassmotrenii zemel'nykh sporov
na territorii g. Iaroslavlia" (April 22, 1992).
[4]Interview, Aleksandr Vasil'evich Vornarev, Chair, Fund of the Yaroslavl City Soviet on
Municipal Property, and Aleksandr Germanovich Savinov, Deputy Chair, Committee of
the Mayor's Office of Yaroslavl on the Administration of Municipal Property, Yaroslavl,
April 29, 1992.
[5]Interview, Lev Leonidovich Kruglikov, Chair, Yaroslavl City Soviet, Yaroslavl, April 28,
1992, and Malyi sovet Iaroslavskogo gorodskogo soveta narodnykh deputatov, "Polozhenie 'O poriadke privatizatsii munitsipal'nykh predpriiatii i imuschchestva g. Iaroslavlia' "
(1991).
[6]Interview, Bobovich, October 14, 1991, and discussions with members of the Yaroslavl
Division of the USSR Union of Architects hosted by Division Chairman Eduard Aleksandrovich Mesian on October 11, 1991, Yaroslavl.
[7]Malyi sovet Iaroslavskogo gorodskogo soveta narodnykh deputatov, "Reshenie No. 65 o
vnesenii dopolnenii i izmenenii v pozhenii o poriadke i usloviikah privatizatsii zhilishchnogo fonda v gorode Iaroslavlia" (April 8, 1992).

20 square meters per resident.[8] Of the city's state-controlled housing stock, 78 percent qualified for free title transfer.[9] Residents of larger apartments would have to pay an additional fee of R698 per square meter (approximately $6 in April 1992). Once title had been obtained, a resident would be able to rent or resell the unit as he or she pleased. Maintenance fees of 0.1 percent of the estimated value of the unit remained strikingly low.[10] Yaroslavtsy, however, were frightened by the specter of ever increasing maintenance fees and taxes in a period of galloping inflation, and they remained loath to privatize.[11] Trade unions opposed the abandonment of a state commitment to free housing.[12] Major enterprises and ministries resisted privatization of their apartment inventory through what they claimed was "yet another round of state expropriation in Russian history."[13]

Claims by "right"-oriented industry officials of "state expropriation" were matched on the "left" of the Russian political spectrum by concern over "municipalization" instead of privatization. Ekaterinburg political activist Alexander Urmanov decried the growing attempt by municipalities to claim ownership of local factories. As Urmanov described the process, "Instead of just selling a factory, a store, a building, or a piece of land to anyone who wants to buy, local officials may offer to lease the property instead. The profit from such 'sales' or leases is often invested by local governments in buying more factories, stores, real estate, or land." Urmanov viewed the process as "creeping counterrevolution."[14] Similar views were evident in Yaroslavl.

The initial three months of housing privatization in Yaroslavl saw the tortuous transfer of only a handful (156) of housing units.[15] Most of those apartments—spacious units located near or on the prestigious Volga Embankment—were most likely inhabited by the old Communist Party elite. Privatization was also popular in the Bragino area, where many middle-level managers reside.[16] Privatization of housing gained

[8]Interview, Kruglikov, April 28, 1992, and interview, Vornarev and Savinov, April 29, 1992.
[9]Interview, Vornarev and Savinov, April 29, 1992.
[10]Ibid.
[11]Interview, Rumiantseva, April 29, 1992.
[12]Interview, Kruglikov, April 28, 1992.
[13]Interview, Vasili Tikhonovich Zheltyakov, Chief Engineer, and Iuzef Iakovlevich Chervnikov, Economic Director, Yaroslavl Motor Works Avtodizel', Yaroslavl, April 29, 1992.
[14]Alexander Urmanov, "The Creeping Counterrevolution in Russia: Local Resistance to Privatization," *Heritage Foundation Backgrounder*, no. 879 (February 6, 1992): 5.
[15]Interview, Vornarev and Savinov, April 29, 1992.
[16]Interview, Rumiantseva, September 4, 1992.

speed throughout April 1992, with 560 units being privatized by the end of the month.[17] Then, during the course of the summer, 3,812 apartments were fully privatized, and the residents of another 6,100 apartments had requested that their units be privatized.[18]

Some officials had predicted such a rapid acceleration during the spring of 1992.[19] What accounts for the fulfillment of their prediction? Leadership, it turns out, made a difference in how Yaroslavl housing privatization programs evolved.

LEADERSHIP MATTERS

Mayor Viktor Volonchunas made a number of television appearances during June and July 1992 in which he made the case for privatization of housing.[20] Volonchunas explained that he was privatizing his own apartment to ensure that he would be able to pass a valuable resource on to his children. He added that the city would continue to maintain apartments at a minimal cost and that the new owners could rent or resell their apartments for income. Pensioners almost immediately began to privatize their apartments in large numbers—both to be able to offer an inheritance to their children and to generate income. Rumors abounded that private firms—such as those headed by the gentleman who proclaimed that "money sings"—were supplementing pensioners' incomes for the right to assume control of apartments after the new owner's death.[21] Others soon followed the pensioners, and by the end of the summer, workers were demanding that their trade unions drop their resistance to privatization and help city officials move the program forward as swiftly as possible.

Leadership mattered in a second way. In expectation of a rising wave of housing privatization, the mini-council established a seven-member independent commission to supervise and manage the transfer of apartment titles.[22] The commission brought together representatives of the

[17]Interview, Kruglikov, May 20, 1992.
[18]Interview, Verbitskii, September 1, 1992.
[19]Interview, Kruglikov, April 28, 1992.
[20]Interview, Rumiantseva, September 4, 1992.
[21]Ibid.; interview, Verbitskii, September 1, 1992.
[22]Malyi sovet Iaroslavskogo gorodskogo soveta narodnykh deputatov, "Reshenie No. 87 o predsedatele nezavisimoi komissii po privatizatsii zhil'ia" (April 22, 1992), and Malyi sovet Iaroslavskogo gorodskogo soveta narodnykh deputatov, "Reshenie No. 94 o sozdanii gorodskoi nezavisimoi komissii po privatizatsii zhilishchnogo fonda v gorode Iaroslavle" (May 6, 1992), together with its accompanying "Polozhenie o nezavisimoi

mayor's office, city council, city housing office, construction associations, major enterprises, and trade unions in an attempt to diminish conflict over the city's housing privatization program. This strategy reflected the city leaders' growing desire to find common ground among competing interests so as to advance their community's position within an increasingly threatening national environment.[23]

At the same time—on May 6, 1992—the mini-council named Iurii Verbitskii as commission chair.[24] Verbitskii, a feisty and savvy politician known for a strong independent (some would argue ornery) streak, was elected to the city council in 1990 with the support of pro-democracy forces. He never shied away from controversy—as was the case when he used his position as chair of that council's Commission on Culture to challenge the transfer of the Church of Elijah the Prophet to the Russian Orthodox Church.

Verbitskii's commission replaced a similar body that had been established to supervise housing privatization by the mayor's office on February 28, 1992, in violation of Russian Federation law.[25] Once under way, meetings of Verbitskii's group were held at least once a week, and the commission claimed responsibility for improving the procedures and standards used in housing privatization. The group's charge was to place the interests of individual citizens and their families at the center of local privatization efforts. Verbitskii reported on the commission's performance both to the city council through its mini-council and directly to the mayor's office.

CALCULATING A FAIR PRICE

Conflicts over valuation of property began almost immediately. The operational legislation used in housing privatization called for the application of a number of variables in the establishment of a price for a given apartment. Verbitskii and his commission determined how these variables were to be applied, and quite naturally, some residents did not agree with their decisions. Appeals were made directly to the mini-council and, eventually, to the city council for adjudication.

komissii po privatizatsii zhilishchnogo fonda v gorode Iaroslavle." Also, interview, Verbitskii, September 1, 1992.
[23]Interview, Kruglikov, May 20, 1992.
[24]Interview, Verbitskii, September 1, 1992.
[25]Ibid.

As Verbitskii explained the procedures, each square meter of Yaroslavl housing space initially had a base value of R698 ($3.40 in September 1992), to which various coefficients are added or subtracted according to building material (+0.5 percent for brick, −0.5 percent for wood, no change for panel structures), size of kitchen space, whether or not there is a balcony, transportation service to the neighborhood, the age of the building, and, of course, location. The values ranged from 85 percent of 698—or R593 for units in wooden structures in poorly serviced districts such as Krasnoperekopskii—to 135 percent (R942) per square meter for the best housing in the city center.[26]

Each citizen received 20 square meters free value, plus an additional 10 square meters for the family unit as a whole, plus 2 square meters for fifteen to twenty years in the work force, 3 square meters for twenty to twenty-five years, 4 square meters for twenty-five to thirty, and 5 square meters for more than thirty years of work service. Hence, a three-member family in which the mother had worked for eighteen years, and the father for twenty-one, and a minor daughter would have had the right to the free transfer of title to an apartment encompassing 60 square meters (20 + 20 + 20) for individual family members, 10 square meters for the family unit, 2 square meters for the mother's labor service, and 3 square meters for the father's labor service, for a total of 75 square meters valued at R698, or a transfer of R52,350 ($255) worth of housing at the September 1992 market rate. If an apartment was valued at more than that amount after the application of the various coefficients mentioned above, the family was to pay the difference. Many residents disputed the application of the coefficients and denied, with some frequency, that location should make any difference in the valuation of their property. Many Yaroslavtsy would have been surprised by the hoary American expression that, in real estate transactions, "location, location, location" matters. Eventually, over three-quarters of the apartment residents in the city qualified for the free transfer of title under this program.

Once an apartment was privatized, a citizen could do with it whatever he or she wanted. Taxes were set at .001 percent of value. Hence, an R40,000 apartment had an R40 tax encumbrance (or $.19). In addition, there was a monthly *kvarplata* for maintenance—also a minimal charge at thirteen kopecks per square meter per month. Eventually, a *tovari-*

[26]Ibid.

shchestvo (fraternal association) was to have been established to handle maintenance after an entire building had been privatized.

MOSCOW REGRESSION AND YAROSLAVL IMMOBILITY

All of the Verbitskii Commission's grand plans came crashing to a halt in early 1993.[27] On January 10, 1993, the Russian Federation Parliament passed a law "supplementing" existing privatization legislation. The changes seemed to be rather benign at the time, but the new law turned out to contain some rather deleterious provisions that undercut local Yaroslavl laws. Given the new signals coming from Moscow during a period of political retrenchment, the Yaroslavl city government turned away from its privatization campaign; popular opinion and citizen action followed suit. If leadership had been critical in launching the privatization initiative the previous spring, the absence of political will subverted the program during the winter.

The January 1993 supplemental legislation fundamentally altered the process of title transfer. All public housing units were to be privatized free of charge. This amendment would appear to have encouraged the privatization process, except that it favored residents of large apartments. The remainder—and majority—of the population had already been entitled to free privatization through the implementation of the various formulas discussed above. The conversion to a "free" privatization strategy had the somewhat perverse effect of convincing public opinion in Yaroslavl that title must be worthless; why else would the state be giving it away?[28] As demand slackened, Yaroslavtsy no longer had to wait in line to initiate privatization of their apartments. Yet, public opinion polls revealed that local citizens were losing interest in the program. Yaroslavtsy became increasingly skeptical of the need to obtain a document—formal title—that did not require a lengthy period of standing in queue in some dark and dank government office.[29] Since the administrative structure implementing the program was intended to be supported on a "pay as you go" basis *(khozraschet)*, the elimination of fees and charges dramatically reduced the financial basis for the city's entire privatization effort.[30]

[27]Ibid., April 14, 1993; interview, Rumiantseva, April 15, 1993.
[28]Interview, Rumiantseva, April 15, 1993.
[29]Ibid.
[30]Interview, Erzhova, April 16, 1993; interview, Verbitskii, September 7, 1993.

The January 1993 legislation went even further, abolishing all housing commissions subordinate to local councils *(sovety)*, including the one
chaired by Iurii Verbitskii. Verbitskii, for his part, reemerged by May
1993 as the chief of a new, four-person Department for the Reconstruction of Historic Structures, housed within the mayor's office.[31] This
move left all supervision of the program to executive branch agencies.
Title documents were no longer to be notarized, undercutting their legal
authority and opening the way for intense battles over competing claims;
these battles would be adjudicated by housing administrators, judges
thought by many to be for sale to the higher bidder. In a surprising
move that went beyond the minimal intent of the Russian Federation
Parliament, the Yaroslavl Mini-Council voted to *return* all funds that
had been collected previously from those who had already privatized
their apartments.[32]

The Parliament's move was but a small skirmish in a larger battle for
power between an emergent antireform majority in the national legislature and the pro-reform Yeltsin administration. It nonetheless reveals
the continued vulnerability of local reformers in the provinces.[33] Verbitskii's independent city commission presided over the privatization of
some fourteen thousand apartments—or almost 10 percent of the city's
total public housing stock—during the nine months of its existence (May
6, 1992–February 1, 1993).[34] It established a number of procedures and
principles that served the city well. Verbitskii and his colleagues attempted to place privatization programs within the context of an overall
housing policy at the local level. In this regard, they had violated one of
the main principles of the local culture of *po tikhon'ku.*

A PROVINCIAL CULTURE OF MODERATE SUCCESS

The nineteenth-century novelist P. I. Mel'nikov (Andrei Perchinskii)
noted at the outset of his tale *In the Forests (V lesakh)* that the people
of the upper Volga are "by turns idle, busy, clever, and cunning."[35] The

---

[31]Information provided to Jeffrey Hahn of Villanova University on a visit to Yaroslavl in
June 1993 and confirmed by interview, Verbitskii, September 7, 1993.
[32]Interview, Verbitskii, April 14, 1993.
[33]This point was emphasized by interview, Erzhova, September 8, 1993.
[34]Ibid.
[35]P. I. Mel'nikov (Andrei Perchinskii), *V lesakh* (Moscow, 1871–74).

primary goal of behavior is to do just enough not to attract attention, while not being so successful as to befall that same fate.

Alla Sevastianova, a Yaroslavl historian who has wrestled with the issue of regional culture in Russia, describes the guiding principle of Yaroslavl life as doing something *po tikhon'ku,* which literally translates as "quietly" but carries with it something of the Washington, D.C., notion of "go along to get along."[36] There is in provincial Russia, to add a slightly different twist, a "culture of moderate success."[37]

The desire to do just enough to satisfy the bosses but not so much to catch their attention underlies much of official behavior surrounding housing privatization in Yaroslavl. For central authorities and their international advisors, the housing privatization campaign was part of a broader initiative to cultivate a middle class in Russian society. Housing ownership was thought to give Russian city dwellers control over their domestic environs for the first time while also transferring a resource that could be built upon to expand private initiative. The transfer of property became a vehicle for contributing simultaneously to the achievement of two distinct reform objectives: breaking the back of government bureaucracies; and establishing a new urban bourgeoisie. Such goals remained far too abstract for most Russian municipal officials, let alone for many inhabitants of public housing across Russia. For the typical Russian citizen, daily survival and rather imprecise calculations of economic costs and benefits proved to be far more salient when approaching the privatization issue.

City and provincial Yaroslavl officials did not try to reconceptualize central initiatives, nor did they attempt to thwart central will. When national powers supported reform-oriented initiatives such as housing privatization, so too did local officials. When the signals emanating from Moscow were somehow contradictory, the impetus for reform dissolved. The result is an example of regional policy implementation that is neither ahead of nor behind the pack. Yaroslavl experience in this area—as in many others—is merely "typical," but never "exemplary."[38] It is not surprising, therefore, that privatization plans in Yaroslavl were based on

[36]Interview, Alla Sevastianova, Professor of History, Yaroslavl State University, Yaroslavl, April 13, 1993.
[37]Glazychev, "Social Change in Provincial Russian Towns."
[38]Yaroslavl's unexceptional performance in post-Soviet era reform is explored in Kathryn Stoner-Weiss, "Local Heroes: Political Exchange and Regional Government Performance in Post-Communist Russia" (Ph.D. diss., Harvard University, 1994).

proposals emanating from Moscow and St. Petersburg. Local politicians, it should also be noted, sent busloads of Yaroslavl officials to Nizhnii Novgorod when that city caught favor among reformers—although they returned less than impressed.[39]

Despite moderate success, housing privatization programs were crippled in Yaroslavl and elsewhere from their very inception. The rush to initiate privatization programs left a number of legal and administrative loose ends in need of careful attention. Financial institutions never developed, thereby inhibiting the emergence of a viable housing market including the resale of privatized properties. Even such straightforward measures as the creation of a municipal data base of housing sales were never accomplished.[40] Nadezhda Erzhova, the head of the Mayor's Housing Privatization Office, noted in frustration throughout 1993 that there was no national housing policy and, furthermore, that privatization programs were "meaningless" without such a program.[41]

WHO PRIVATIZED THEIR APARTMENTS FIRST?

Housing privatization continued in Yaroslavl in 1993, though at a substantially reduced pace. By April 4, 1993, 22,422 apartments had been privatized (for overview on March 1, 1993, see Table 2), and another 4,445 requests were being processed (recall that only 156 had been privatized just a year before).[42] In all, some 30,000 units were transferred from municipal to private ownership before the collapse of the first republic in late 1993.[43] This figure represented slightly more than one-fifth of the 137,000 apartment units eligible for privatization (an additional 50,000 public housing units were ineligible for the privatization program).[44] Yaroslavl's performance compared unfavorably to that of Mos-

---

[39]Interview, Lisitsyn and Guseev, April 15, 1993; interview, Dmitrii Ponomarev, Specialist, Yaroslavl Regional Information-Analytical Administration, and Aleksei Bushuev, Deputy Chief, Yaroslavl Regional Information-Analytical Administration, Yaroslavl, April 14, 1993; interview, Vornarev, April 13, 1993.

[40]Such a data base is projected to come on-line sometime in 1994. Interview, Erzhova, September 8, 1993.

[41]Ibid., April 16, 1993, and September 8, 1993.

[42]Interview, Rumiantseva, April 15, 1993.

[43]Interview, Erzhova, September 8, 1993.

[44]The slight discrepancies between these figures and those found in Table 2 may be accounted for by the condemnation, construction, and redesignation of municipal apartment buildings during the intervening period. Ibid.

Table 2. *Privatization of housing by urban district, city of Yaroslavl, March 1992–March 1993*

City district	Number of units	% state units	Number privatized	% of city privatized	% in district privatized
Dzerzhinskii	47,560	29%	4,757	22%	10%
Zavolzhskii	26,073	16%	2,582	12%	10%
Kirovskii	25,489	15%	4,797	22%	19%
Krasnoperekopskii	16,502	10%	1,548	8%	9%
Leninskii	23,965	15%	3,890	18%	16%
Fruzhenskii	25,125	15%	3,923	18%	16%
Citywide	164,714	100%	21,497	100%	13%

Sources: Goskomstat RSFSR, Iaroslavskii gorodskoi otdel statistiki, *Statisticheskii biulleten'. Dannye o zhilishchnom fonde goroda Iaroslavlia za 1989 god* (Iaroslavl': February 1990); Meria goroda Iaroslavlia, Otdel privatizatsii zhil'ia, "Dannye po privatizatsii zhil'ia grazhdanami g. Iaroslavlia za period s 01.03.92 po 26.03.93."

cow, where nearly 33 percent of the municipal housing stock had been privatized at that time.

Those citizens requesting title of their apartments tended to fall into two distinct groups: those who were privileged; and pensioners who required new sources of income.[45] Such trends are evident in a district-by-district accounting of housing privatization for the period from March 1992 to March 1993 (Table 2). According to those data, the Kirovskii District of central Yaroslavl—which is the venue of much of the housing occupied by the old Communist Party *apparat*—tied with the Dzerzhinskii District in terms of its percentage of the privatized housing stock for the entire city and surpassed all other districts in terms of the percentage of its own housing stock that had been privatized. The large numbers of units privatized in the Dzerzhinskii District were primarily in the Bragino area, which was home to many middle-level managers. More proletarian districts—such as the Krasnoperekopskii—straggled behind. The relatively small number of privatized apartments in the Zavolzhskii District is somewhat deceptive, since many cooperative apartment buildings were built together with state housing when the area was developed during the 1980s. As a result, the number of Za-

[45]Ibid., September 8, 1993, and April 16, 1993.

volzhskii residents living in nonstate housing remained among the city's highest.

By mid-1993, a third group of privatizers had emerged: those Yaroslavtsy who were leaving town or were dividing up their property among family members.[46] Hence, Yaroslavl residents were prepared to privatize their apartments when they perceived a clear reason to do so: residents of premier buildings benefiting from the relatively high valuation of their apartments, pensioners requiring supplemental incomes, migrants departing for other towns and regions, etc. The typical Yaroslavets, however, conjectured that there would be little gain from the additional responsibilities of ownership at a time of political and economic uncertainty.

In addition to the privatization of municipal housing, Verbitskii's commission worked on a contract basis to manage the privatization of factory housing. Managers at several industrial enterprises were beginning to feel the pressures of rising prices and tightening credits induced by Russia's attempt at "shock therapy," or rapid economic reform. Looking for ways to reduce overhead, enterprise managers began to consider, for the first time, relinquishing control over factory housing. By releasing their housing to private control, some managers hoped to stave off the bankruptcies that were thought to be looming on the horizon in late 1992.[47] The Russian Federation government's failure to sustain tight credits in the industrial sector later ended this managerial fascination with shedding paternalistic responsibility for the care, feeding, and housing of factory workers and their families.

Beyond privatization of existing housing, state construction firms in Yaroslavl have begun building new apartments farther from the city center with the intention of offering the new units at market-based rents.[48] City officials have been exploring the possibilities for offering older buildings to construction trusts for restoration, although Russian Federation guidelines prohibit privatization of communal (multifamily) apartments and of units located within historic districts. Even if pursued, the sale of inhabited buildings to new owners will require the approval of *all* residents.[49]

[46]Ibid., September 8, 1993.
[47]Interview, Rumiantseva, September 4, 1992; Interview, Verbitskii, September 1, 1992.
[48]Interview, Vornarev and Savinov, April 29, 1992.
[49]Ibid.

LOCAL HOUSING PRIVATIZATION PROGRAMS: AN EVALUATION

Why did Yaroslavtsy respond to privatization initiatives in the housing sphere in such a muddled manner?[50] For those who already lived in the city's better apartments, any short-term risk in housing privatization was more than offset by the potential long-term gain accrued by obtaining an asset that could be capitalized in some future market-oriented Russian economy. The *nomenklatura* moved quickly to secure their previous advantage in the housing sector and privatized their apartments.

Pensioners, for their part, faced an immediate cash crunch as their already modest monthly payments from the state lost nearly all value under the crushing weight of rampant inflation. Privatization offered them an immediate opportunity to capitalize an asset. Many pensioners privatized without delay.

Those Yaroslavtsy who were forced to move or leave town similarly sought to privatize their apartments. Such an action diminished the cumbersome administrative procedures otherwise required to change one's place of residence.

For the majority of city residents, however, longer-term family stability demanded the development of new survival strategies. Subsidized municipal housing costs remained of secondary concern in the face of impending unemployment until Mayor Volonchunas launched his summer 1992 privatization campaign. That effort demonstrated the potential benefits of apartment ownership. Volonchunas thus managed to elevate the housing issue in the survival hierarchy. Most Yaroslavtsy intended to privatize their apartments but simply did not manage to initiate the process before the laws shifted yet again.

The January 1993 legislative reforms, innocent though they may appear to have been at first glance, dramatically altered cost and benefit calculations. These amendments signified a continuing political battle that threatened reform initiatives more generally. Under these circumstances, being a "greedy privatizer" might not be a desirable label in the years to come. If reform continued, the costs of apartment maintenance would rise as well. A resident's most rational option, once again, was to remain in municipal-controlled housing until the political situation stabilized.

[50] I would like to acknowledge the insights that I gained about citizen reaction to the privatization process from conversations and correspondence with Steven Solnick.

The situation in Yaroslavl was rather different from that in Moscow and St. Petersburg, where foreign and native entrepreneurs were driving housing costs up to world levels. The long-term hazard of being dangerously politically incorrect was more than offset by the huge profits to be gained from rental or sale of apartment space in the Russian Federation's two largest metropolitan centers. So far as provincial Russians were concerned, proceeding *po tikhon'ku* remained the most advantageous survival strategy.

AUCTIONING OFF STATE TRADE

Privatization of trade moved along more expeditiously than the selling off of public housing. Meanwhile, the privatization of the industrial enterprises—in Yaroslavl as in many other Russian cities—lagged behind all other privatization efforts.[51]

Working within standards established in October 1991 by the Yaroslavl City Council, local officials offered municipally owned enterprises for sale after 50 percent of the enterprise work force had agreed through a referendum and subsequent confirmation by petition.[52] Local authorities revised procedures incessantly, fostering ever greater uncertainty about the appropriate measures for transferring ownership of state enterprises to private hands.[53] Deviously complex and ever changing registration procedures demanded the intervention of lawyers and financial officers even after approval had been granted by both enterprise employees and city agencies following a two-stage review.[54]

As in many other Russian cities, political stalemate in Yaroslavl between entrenched bureaucrats from the old regime and more liberal, elected legislators and mayors initially created an atmosphere that can be described only as hostile to privatization.[55] Local officials responsible

[51]Interview, Vornarev and Savinov, April 29, 1992.

[52]Malyi sovet Iaroslavskogo gorodskogo soveta narodnykh deputatov, "Polozhenie 'O poriadke privatizatsii munitsipal'nykh predpriiatii i imushchestva g. Iaroslavlia' " (1991).

[53]See, for example, Malyi sovet Iaroslavskogo gorodskogo soveta narodnykh deputatov, "Reshenie No. 20 o privatizatsii munitsipal'nykh predpriiatii i imushchestva g. Iaroslavlia na 1992 god" (February 13, 1992), and Malyi sovet Iaroslavskogo gorodskogo soveta narodnykh deputatov, "Reshenie No. 75 o vnesenii izmenenii i dopolnenii v reshenie malogo soveta No. 20 ot 13.02.92 g. o privatizatsii munitsipal'nykh predpriiatii i imushchestva g. Iaroslavlia" (April 22, 1992).

[54]Interview, Vornarev and Savinov, April 29, 1992.

[55]Readers may wish to compare this account of privatization initiatives in Yaroslavl with the account provided by Lynn D. Nelson and Irina Y. Kuzes of similar efforts in Moscow, Ekaterinburg, Voronezh, and Smolensk. See Lynn D. Nelson and Irina Y. Kuzes, *Property*

for the program worked hard to foster visibly successful entrepreneurial pioneers to spur on others to seek title over their stores, enterprises, and other workplaces. Aleksandr Vornarev, the chair of the Yaroslavl City Soviet Fund on Municipal Property, reported that 110 commercial properties were sold at ten auctions during 1992: 97 of 359 trade establishments, 11 of 40 food outlets, and 2 of 63 service providers. Approximately one-third of the sales involved the purchase of both leases and real property, usually in the form of commercial space. The city auctioned off leasing arrangements in two-thirds of the sales. Of these auctions, 80 percent had some sort of condition attached—such as a commitment to retain all store employees for a set period of time or to continue sales of a particular product. The remaining properties were offered to buyers for any purpose. Vornarev contended that approximately two-thirds of the purchasers were employee collectives and another quarter were private firms, with the balance being individual owners.[56] All but one sale was to local owners, the single exception being an owner who was from a Baltic state but who had relatives in Yaroslavl.

Only a handful of bidders participated in early auctions, but by the fall of 1992, a number of new entrepreneurs had joined in the bidding. The city shifted to weekly auctions of municipal stores and enterprises at that time.[57] Newspaper advertisements announcing the availability of facilities for privatization by auction increased participation in the program.[58] Interest continued to grow throughout early 1993, when the changing political climate and the growing difficulties imposed by rising inflation began to take their toll on buyer interest.[59] Auctions fell back to once a month. Prices continued to vary over time and location, with a premium being placed by bidders on central location. A small

---

[56]Interview, Vornarev, September 1, 1992, and April 13, 1993.

to the People: The Struggle for Radical Economic Reform in Russia (Armonk, N.Y.: M. E. Sharpe, 1994).

[57]Although this study focuses on privatization of municipal property, a similar program was initiated at the same time for the privatization of regional *(oblastnogo)* property and encountered many of the same problems (Malyi sovet Iaroslavskogo gorodskogo soveta narodnykh deputatov, "Reshenie No. 198 ob otchete predsedatelia komiteta po upravleniiu gosimushchestvom po ispolneniiu programmy privatizatsii gosudarstvennykh i munitsipal'nykh predpriiatii Iaroslavskoi oblasti na 1992 g. ot 30 sentiabria").

[58]See, for example, "Fond munitsipal'nogo imushchestva g. Iaroslavlia ob"iavliaet torgi na 20 avgusta 1992 sleduiushchikh predpriiatii," *Gorodskie novosti,* July 23, 1992, p. 2, and "Fond munitsipal'nogo imushchestva g. Iaroslavlia ob"iavliaet torgi na 29 sentiabria," *Gorodskie novosti,* August 27, 1992, p. 4.

[59]Interview, Vornarev, April 13, 1993.

storefront in the center city, for example, sold in the same August 1992 auction for two-thirds of the price of a large vegetable store in Bragino.[60]

The Yaroslavl program for privatizing municipal enterprises (primarily in trade) continued to move along in fits and starts throughout the waning weeks of the first republic.[61] One auction of seven food stores held on May 20, 1993, was restricted to organizations with demonstrated experience in food processing (e.g., collective and state farms). This move was part of a more general effort by city officials to attach binding conditions to a sale or lease of commercial establishments, ensuring that the new proprietors would better serve their employees and communities.

The number of auctions increased to two per month in May and July. Approximately 80 percent of all municipal-controlled stores in Yaroslavl had been privatized before the collapse of the first republic (as compared with some 60 percent in Moscow at the same time).[62] Nearly half of the sales were to those labor collectives already working in a given establishment, so that the initial post-Soviet wave of privatization in trade was not necessarily producing new management structures. Undercapitalization continued to plague various trade organizations, with new owners frequently unable to upgrade operations following their purchase of a facility. Inflation similarly continued to cripple investment plans.

THE ZIGS AND ZAGS OF REFORM

Much to the chagrin of local authorities, auction prices fell off after their peak at the July 13, 1993, sale.[63] Various levels of government divided up program revenues, so that local politicians had become quite keen on holding auctions to privatize trade. Of the R60 million (nearly $150,000 at the end of 1992) collected by the auctions, 45 percent went to the Yaroslavl Regional Administration, 25 percent to Yaroslavl city coffers, and 20 percent to the Russian Federation government, with the remainder being divided evenly between the two municipal agencies run-

---

[60]Ibid., September 1, 1992.

[61]Information on the program's evolution in 1993 was provided by ibid., April 13, 1993, and interview, Ivan Ivanovich Komarev, Chief of the Department of Privatization of Municipal Property for Yaroslavl City, Yaroslavl, September 8, 1993.

[62]Interview, Iurii Mikhailovich Samoikin, Deputy Chief, Moscow Division of the Russian Federation State Committee for Anti-Monopoly Policy and for the Promotion of New Economic Structures, Moscow, September 3, 1993.

[63]Interview, Komarev, September 8, 1993.

ning the program.[64] Up to 40 percent of the purchase could be paid in Russian Federation privatization vouchers, but the rest of the payment had to be made in cash. This requirement of at least 60 percent paid in cash undercut the capacity of new entrepreneurs to invest further in their businesses. Insufficient capital reserves, intense municipal regulation, and skepticism about the future combined to frustrate the program.[65]

The pattern that developed in Yaroslavl of accelerating privatization in the service sector during 1992 followed by deceleration in early 1993 appears to have been repeated in other Russian communities. Yaroslavl is more typical than exemplary. The St. Petersburg city government privatized 550 stores in household services, 336 in food services, and 1,054 in trade during the first eleven months of 1992—with more being privatized later in the year than at the beginning.[66] The absolute numbers of privatized enterprises were even higher in Moscow.[67] Meanwhile, some 600 large enterprises and 40,000 small businesses were privatized throughout Russia during 1992.[68]

Many politicians in a variety of communities such as St. Petersburg, Moscow, Ekaterinburg, and Yaroslavl have been exasperated by the complexity of the privatization issue. Confronting escalating municipal budgets, they readily acknowledge the need to free their cities of responsibility for maintaining housing. A few recognize the psychological, economic, and political value of home and store ownership. Some national trade union leaders—long opponents of housing privatization— are beginning to praise, rather grudgingly, the psychological empowerment of privatization.[69] Yet, nearly everyone involved in the process predicts endless conflicts and disputes in an increasingly contentious society that continues to view such goods as housing as entitlements essentially provided by the state at little or no cost to itself and at little or no cost to the consumer.[70]

[64]Interview, Vornarev, April 13, 1993.
[65]Interview, Leonid Mozeiko, President, Yartec Business Center, Yaroslavl, April 16, 1993.
[66]IA 'Severo-Zapad', "Itogi privatizatsii v Peterburge," *Nezavisimaia gazeta*, December 15, 1992, p. 4.
[67]Interview, Samoikin, September 3, 1993.
[68]Keith Bush, "Progress of Russian Privatization," *RFE/RL Daily Report*, no. 1 (January 4, 1993): 1.
[69]I. Nevinnaia, "Osobniaki budut u bogatykh," *Trud*, August 28, 1992, p. 3.
[70]Galina Yeremicheva and Nani Kulish Boyce present sociological data that underscore the significance of housing as a free good to Russians in G. Yeremicheva and N. K. Boyce, "Privatization of Housing in St. Petersburg, Russia," *Environment and Planning Annual* (United Kingdom), 1992, pp. 177–80.

BUILDING THE SUBURBAN DREAM

A private housing sector existed in Russia throughout the Soviet period.[71] Of the Russian Federation's urbanites in June 1990, 15 percent lived in "housing owned by individual citizens," including 12 percent inhabiting "single-family dwellings."[72] These were almost exclusively overcrowded and poorly serviced private wooden houses. In addition, a limited but vibrant cooperative apartment market existed in nearly every Russian city. Although the percentage of all Soviet-period urban housing in cooperatives was a low 3.8 percent in the Russian Federation at the end of 1990, this housing stock had long provided an important alternative to management by state agencies.[73] By 1993, cooperative associations in Moscow were beginning to band together to protect mutual interests.[74] In Yaroslavl, both the private and the cooperative housing sectors are likely to expand regardless of the disposition of the city's public housing.

Changes in Russian Federation legislation during 1991 permitted the construction of new private homes in urban areas for the first time since 1961.[75] A few rather substantial single-family dwellings have been constructed in Yaroslavl, with the starting price of a three- to five-room, one- to two-story brick house originally running between R200,000 and 500,000 at the end of 1991 (between U.S. $5,000 and $12,500 at the time).[76] New homes were being built on lots within previously existing settlements of wooden houses in order to facilitate provision of city services (Figure 16). This practice brought some of the city's richest and poorest residents into immediate proximity. Long-time residents quickly

---

[71]For Western accounts of Soviet-era urban housing practices, see A. J. DiMaio, *Soviet Urban Housing: Problems and Policies* (New York: Praeger, 1974); Henry W. Morton, "Who Gets What, When, and How? Housing in the Soviet Union," *Soviet Studies* 31, no. 2 (1980): 235–59; Henry W. Morton, "Housing in the Soviet Union," *Academy of Political Science Proceedings* 35, no. 3 (1984); and Carol Nichemias, "The Impact of Soviet Housing Policy on Housing Conditions in Soviet Cities: The Uneven Push from Moscow," *Urban Studies* 18, no. 1 (1981).

[72]Raymond J. Struyk et al., *Implementing Housing Allowances in Russia: Rationalizing the Rental Sector* (Washington, D.C.: Urban Institute, 1993), p. 14.

[73]Hanson, Kosareva, and Struyk, "Housing Reform in the Russian Federation," pp. 1–2.

[74]Vladimir Moiseev, "Istoriia ZhSK mozhet zavershit'sia v Rossii," *Nezavisimaia gazeta*, January 11, 1993, p. 6.

[75]Discussion with members of the Yaroslavl Division of the USSR Union of Architects hosted by Division Chairman Eduard Aleksandrovich Mesian, Yaroslavl, October 11, 1991.

[76]Cost estimates rose and fell according to the official position of the interlocutor. Those with more responsible positions—and perhaps more removed from the rough-and-tumble world of Yaroslavl construction practices—tended to quote lower prices.

Figure 16. A new single-family house in Yaroslavl, 1991. Photograph by Blair A. Ruble.

expressed dissatisfaction with their haughty new neighbors, and some local officials anticipated increasing social tensions from these arrangements.[77] Such programs were expanding quickly, with new districts being set aside for single-family housing construction quite far from previously existing districts—in newly developed areas to the northeast, southeast, and west.[78] Architects in Yaroslavl and elsewhere in Russia are delighted to have the novel experience of working closely with private clients to design single-family dwellings.[79]

The newly emerging Russian private housing industry hit its stride

[77]The author witnessed one such heated exchange between city officials and local residents over four new brick houses in Yaroslavl during a city tour organized by Arkady Romanovich Bobovich, Chief Architect, Yaroslavl City Executive Committee, and Tatiana Pavlovna Rumiantseva, Director, Public Opinion Research Center, Yaroslavl City Soviet, on October 14, 1991. No issues were resolved before the visiting dignitaries were forced to flee the scene.

[78]Interview, Bobovich, September 1, 1992.

[79]See, for example, A. Ts. Dychinskii, "Chelovek i sreda obitaniia," *St. Peterburgskaia panorama*, no. 9 (1992): 26–29. Dychinskii was the chief architect of the Leningrad Region at the time the article appeared.

during mid-1993.[80] Private construction contractors were working with local state and collective farms by that time to create a rough-and-tumble market for newly built private homes, especially in the Moscow Region but also in the neighboring Yaroslavl Region. As the *New York Times* reported in August of that year, "The vast majority of Russian home buyers are in for a very different experience from that of their American counterparts. There is no such thing as a mortgage—or even a checking account—so people pay cash. For those who can't afford to plop down enough to buy a finished house, building a home is fraught with head-aches."[81] Nevertheless, a thriving do-it-yourself industry emerged, offering all sorts of hardware and building materials; Russians had long ago learned how to wend their way through a tortuous supply and regulatory system to construct their own dachas (country homes).[82]

Legal scholars credited the new housing market to the legalization of land sales, changes in the legal status of state and collective farms (which permitted farms to "hand out" lots), and the repeal of various building code limits on farmhouses.[83] Moscow's growing post-Soviet bourgeoisie created an almost insatiable demand for the new houses in nearby areas.

The private housing boom of 1993 spread to Yaroslavl as well, though in somewhat muted form. The network of habitation spread farther and farther out from the city of Yaroslavl into the surrounding countryside of the Yaroslavl Region. The physical contours of the city began to be transformed in response to changes in the underlying economic system accompanying the collapse of Soviet-era economic planning and management. Building sites, for example, were staked out near Korovniki directly across the Kotorosl' River from central Yaroslavl. The area—which is dominated by the seventeenth-century churches of St. John Chrysostom and the Vladimir Mother of God on one side[84] and a large eighteenth-century prison built by Catherine the Great on the other—had long been run down and dispossessed by local authorities. The sad home to dozens of poor families for decades, the area's cheerless

---

[80]Ann Imse, "A Housing Boom Remakes the Russian Landscape," *New York Times*, August 29, 1993, p. F5.

[81]Ibid.

[82]For an informative account of precisely what "do-it-yourself" dacha construction means, see Aleksandr Vysokovskii, "Will Domesticity Return?," in Brumfield and Ruble, *Russian Housing in the Modern Age*, pp. 271–308.

[83]Imse, "A Housing Boom Remakes the Russian Landscape."

[84]Brumfield discusses the importance of these churches for the development of Russian ecclesiastical architecture during the second half of the seventeenth century in his monumental volume *A History of Russian Architecture*, pp. 156–59.

Figure 17. The author at the site of a new housing development in Korovniki, 1993. Photograph by Kathryn Stoner-Weiss.

little vegetable market was about to house some of Yaroslavl's richest residents (Figure 17). New winners and old losers were coming to live cheek by jowl as a new social order became visibly evident in the evolving physical structure of the post-Soviet city.

Impending privatization similarly prompted changes in public-sector housing.[85] Industrial enterprises such as the Avtodizel' Motor Works also undertook the design and construction of single-family dwellings for their workers. Such programs will undoubtedly influence how Yaroslavtsy live their lives and will be discussed later in this volume.

The Architectural Administration of the Yaroslavl City Executive Committee also attempted to be more creative in developing its housing projects. The first apartment house designed exclusively for pensioners, for example, opened in early 1993 on a downtown site opposite the Yaroslavl Pedagogical Institute just behind Youth Square. The building,

[85]Interview, Bobovich, October 14, 1991.

Figure 18. A new apartment house for pensioners, near Youth Square, 1993. Photograph by Blair A. Ruble.

which contains thirty-four one-room apartments with large kitchens, was constructed in anticipation of the displacement of retirees following the expected rise of housing costs in the wake of privatization. The final structure was perhaps the most architecturally successful building constructed in the city in years—a stucco exterior that would be at home nestled into any Nordic streetscape (Figure 18). It is not surprising that the building won awards for being one of the best Russian buildings constructed in 1992.[86]

THE FOREIGNERS ARRIVE

Lacking experience with a private housing market, Yaroslavl officials sought advice and investment from abroad. Housing ranked high among international technical-assistance programs—especially housing for decommissioned military officers and enlisted personnel. In Yaroslavl, re-

[86]Ibid., April 15, 1993.

gional and city managers became increasingly concerned about creating a quality infrastructure for private houses owned by a broader spectrum of local society. Interest in foreign investment and assistance grew with the realization that private housing would be an essential component to any successful effort to create a local bourgeoisie. A local bourgeoisie, some politicians argued, was a sine qua non for a more stable political environment. A few of the more flamboyant political figures of the city and the region eyed future election campaigns. Earning credit for housing large numbers of Yaroslavl voters would be a considerable asset in Russia's new electoral politics. Much to local surprise, American and French construction firms arrived with blueprints in hand, almost on cue.

American investors zeroed in on a rural housing project near Pereslavl-Zalesski even before the end of the Soviet era. Yaroslavl officials initially praised the Yankee initiative, which was located on the fringes of the Moscow megalopolis yet within the Yaroslavl Region. Begun in September 1990 as a joint venture, the Pereslavl project moved toward construction in mid-1992 under the auspices of the American construction firm RADVA, based in Radford, Virginia.[87] RADVA President Luther Dickens initially anticipated that the firm's panel factory would be fully operational in 1993, with suburban-style American houses being available for sale shortly thereafter.[88] Unfortunately, various difficulties inherent in the conduct of business in Russia during this period delayed the start-up of construction by RADVA.[89] Local officials became increasingly concerned about the apparent unwillingness of the American company to adapt floor plans and building materials to local taste and need. City Chief Architect Arkady Bobovich was curious, for example, to see how well American drywall would survive "a good, old-fashioned Russian family brawl."[90] The American attitude, many Yaroslavtsy complained, seemed to be that Russians would just have to learn how to live *po amerikanskomu.*

The Phoenix construction company from France also entered the Ya-

[87]Ibid., September 1, 1992. Also see Iu. Sevriukov, "Mister Dikkens iz Radforda," *Severnyi krai,* August 8, 1992, p. 2, and D. Sevriukov, "Zhit', kak v shtatakh," *Zolotoe kol'tso,* August 13, 1992, p. 1.
[88]Personal correspondence with Luther I. Dickens, President, RADVA Corporation of Radford, Virginia, October 16, 1992.
[89]Interview, Guseev, June 18, 1993.
[90]Interview, Bobovich, September 9, 1993.

roslavl housing market, building a plant during 1993 in nearby Rybinsk to produce ten thousand prefabricated homes a year.[91] Some of these "cottages" would be placed in the city of Yaroslavl. Once again, a number of start-up difficulties delayed production. However, the French were more sensitive than their American competitors to local expectations. Floor plans were adapted to incorporate mud rooms and storage areas for vegetables, for example.[92] Kitchen areas were expanded in the new blueprints, and bedrooms were reduced in size. Phoenix officials and their Yaroslavl partners initiated negotiations with Moscow private banks to establish financing programs to expand the available market for the homes.

The first models were open for inspection in early October 1993.[93] In late October, Governor Anatolii Lisitsyn called a press conference to discuss the Phoenix project.[94] Lisitsyn proudly revealed that the Nizhnii Novgorod Regional Administration was joining in the backing of public-supported loans for individual owners of Phoenix houses. Eventually, production levels are planned to surpass the six thousand prefabricated apartment units that were built throughout the region annually between 1984 and 1986.[95] Regional officials anticipate that the French company will be able to create a national market for the homes and create new jobs for local workers. They also view such programs as a new strategy for increasing the local housing stock.[96]

The new housing market in Yaroslavl has been gravely hindered by the absence of financial institutions.[97] Demand has been growing in Russia for a functioning mortgage market that can extend credit to potential home owners on a commercial basis.[98] Otherwise, privatization will re-

[91] Aleksandr Bekker, "Iaroslavl' ishchet mesto v zhizni," *Segodnia*, July 6, 1993, p. 3; interview, Lisitsyn and Guseev, April 15, 1993.

[92] Interview, Bobovich, September 9, 1993; A. Pushkarnaia, "Frantsuzskii dom v rossiiskom inter'ere," *Severnyi krai*, September 11, 1993, p. 1.

[93] Pushkarnaia, "Frantsuzskii dom v rossiiskom inter'ere."

[94] "V oblastnoi administratsii 'Feniks'—eshche ne sinitsa v ruke. No i ne zhuravl' v nebe," *Severnyi krai*, October 27, 1993, p. 1.

[95] Interview, Bobovich, April 15, 1993.

[96] Ibid., September 1, 1992.

[97] Interview, Eduard Aleksandrovich Mesian, Chairman, Yaroslavl Division of the USSR Union of Architects, Yaroslavl, September 2, 1992. For an expanded discussion of this issue in relation to St. Petersburg, see N. A. Malinina and Iu. A. Iakovleva, "Rossiiskii rynok zhil'ia," *S.-Peterburgskaia panorama*, 1992, no. 7, p. 7.

[98] Chuck Hanson and Raymond Struyk, "USAID Technical Assistance Strategy for the Russian Federation in the Shelter Sector," *Urban Institute International Activities Center Research Paper* (Washington, D.C.: Urban Institute, 1992 [May]), pp. 9–10; Struyk et al., *Implementing Housing Allowances in Russia*, pp. 34–36.

main nothing more than a meaningless transfer of state obligations to a Russian citizenry lacking the basic resources required to accept such responsibilities. Preliminary interest in just the promise of an expanding private housing market indicates that the privatization of housing—and perhaps of urban land later on—will dramatically reshape the politics of urban space in Yaroslavl. Money already meant a great deal throughout the local housing market even as the first republic came to a fiery end in Moscow on October 3–4, 1993.

3

Preservation battles

The preservation of notable buildings has stood at the center of the politics of property in Yaroslavl for some time. The city's historic character has long been a central fact of local life, establishing narrow physical constraints on economic development. German invaders and Red Army defenders never wiped clean the cityscape of Yaroslavl, as they did those of Soviet frontline towns. Many historic structures—especially religious buildings—were destroyed during various Soviet-era antireligious or large-scale construction campaigns, but such destruction failed to eradicate the prerevolutionary town. Yaroslavl's rich inventory of historic buildings could not—and cannot—be ignored.

Several additional factors beyond the mere physical legacy of past generations have placed preservation issues at the top of the local political agenda. Preservation movements—together with environmental activism—remained among the few areas open to grass-roots political initiative during the Khrushchev and Brezhnev regimes.[1] Many leaders of the Gorbachev-era democratic movement in Yaroslavl, as in several other Soviet towns and cities, began their political careers by rallying behind preservation causes.

The disposition of Yaroslavl's particularly large number of historic religious structures—especially Orthodox churches and monasteries—provoked vociferous disputes over the appropriate role of religious in-

[1] The battles in St. Petersburg (then Leningrad) surrounding the renovation of the Astoria Hotel and the Hotel Angletera during the spring of 1987, for example, became the founding event of the democratic movement that would overthrow the city's power structure in elections held two and three years later (Interview, Elena Zelinskaia, Member, Leningrad People's Front, Washington, D.C., May 14, 1990). The controversies surrounding the Astoria-Angletera renovation are described in Ruble, *Leningrad*, pp. 89–93.

stitutions in post-Soviet Russian life. The appearance of interested foreign investors similarly prompted public debate over the place of Russia and Russian culture in a more open and penetrable world. Emotional struggles over the optimal balance between community interests and individual property rights were played out in Yaroslavl courtrooms as local politicians, business leaders, and preservation activists were pitted against one another over the right to establish new heritage regulations. As in other elements of city building under Russia's first post-Soviet republic, money began to matter as never before.

THE DIALECTICS OF PRESERVATION

The decision to preserve historic buildings and neighborhoods within rapidly changing surroundings seeks both to limit the pace of change and to provide recognizable outposts within an increasingly alien environment. Historic preservation programs around the world have emerged at times as powerful shields of wealth and privilege.[2] Nevertheless, many local elites look to preservation programs as an engine of economic change. By drawing on historic urban tableaux to provide what M. Christine Boyer has called "spectacles of stimulation," developers aspire to liberate surplus capital from the wallets of bourgeois revelers who have grown bored with the contemporary world.[3]

Tourism—perhaps the largest and most international of all postindustrial economic sectors—flourishes within the comfortable confines of traditional urban space. Tourism has profoundly altered how our cities look and function. Deyan Sudjic did not stretch credulity when he observed, "As a force for social change, tourism has had an impact of the same order as the industrial revolution."[4] The "city of production" has become, in the words of French urban specialist Guy Burgel, a "city of consumption."[5] Yet, Sudjic and Burgel write of a revolution that, until

---

[2]For an interesting contrast to the situation in Russia, see Jorge E. Hardoy and Margarita Gutman, "The Role of Municipal Government in the Protection of Historic Centres in Latin American Cities," *Environment and Urbanization* 3, no. 1 (April 1991): 96–108. The Latin American comparison is particularly apt given the interest in preservation efforts and in the ensuing tourism as a mechanism through which impoverished municipal administrations can capture foreign investment and capital directly, without the interference of national governments.

[3]M. Christine Boyer, "Cities for Sale: Merchandising History at South Street Seaport," in Michael Sorkin, ed., *Variations on a Theme Park: The New American City and the End of Public Space* (New York: Hill and Wang/Noonday Press, 1992), pp. 181–204 (186).

[4]Deyan Sudjic, *The 100 Mile City* (San Diego: Harcourt Brace, 1992), p. 264.

[5]Guy Burgel, *La Ville Aujourd'hui* (Paris: Hachette, 1993), pp. 119–29.

quite recently, has largely bypassed Russia. With tourism now on local agendas, citizens and governments in Yaroslavl, as well as in other historic Russian towns and cities, must reconsider the goals of historic preservation efforts.

Communities around the world pursue historic preservation programs for multiple and even contradictory ends, seeking both to limit the impact of the outside world and to attract outside investment. This inconsistency demands decision processes that are predicated on conflict. The variance in values and goals underlying historic preservation advocacy within a community provides a fortuitous laboratory for research focusing on how residents conceive their community and how such conceptions change over time. The issue of historic preservation thus suggests a number of policy issues that will confront Yaroslavl leaders in the years to come as they seek to redefine urban space in the post-Soviet era.

Many politically active citizens in Yaroslavl—and, it should be noted, in other historic Russian cities—view preservation as unassailably positive. This impulse is frequently driven by a distinctively Russian appreciation of the picturesque, the asymmetrical, and the unexpected in the built environment—qualities that have been worn away by the massive prefabricated structures built over the past three decades.[6] This view combines with an emotional attachment to a pre-Soviet Russian past, as is evident in the recent return of tsarist symbols (the tricolor flag, the double-headed eagle, etc.). At the core, such critiques rest on a rejection—one shared well beyond Russia—of modernist design principles.

YAROSLAVL'S BATTLE FOR A PRESERVATION ZONE

The historic preservation movement has been active in Russia for some time.[7] Initially, efforts were undertaken to preserve single buildings of historic or aesthetic merit. Some of the most striking buildings in Yaroslavl, such as the magnificent seventeenth-century Church of Elijah the Prophet, were restored as individual historical and cultural monuments.[8]

---

[6]For but a single, particularly eloquent example of this sentiment, see S. P. Zavarikhin, "Progulka po prospektu prosveshcheniia," *Leningradskaia panorama*, no. 9 (1986): 20–23.

[7]One overview of the movement may be found in R. A. French, "Conserving the Past in Soviet Cities," *Kennan Institute Occasional Paper No. 235* (Washington, D.C.: Kennan Institute for Advanced Russian Studies/Woodrow Wilson International Center for Scholars, 1990).

[8]This church is discussed in Brumfield, *A History of Russian Architecture*, pp. 145–47, and in Brumfield, *Lost Russia*.

The task of preserving individual structures is compounded in the Russian case by the importance in the national architectural tradition—and most especially in ecclesiastical design—of the relationship of the ensemble to its surroundings. The setting of a particular building may be its most critical compositional element. In such instances, preservation of an individual building without care for the total site greatly diminishes its aesthetic value.[9] Such artistic considerations may be seen, for example, in a particularly noxious Soviet-era town that was constructed up to the walls of the historic Sergeev Posad monastery (renamed "Zagorsk," after a revolutionary hero, during the Soviet period).

By the 1970s, Russian architects, planners, and, somewhat later, an activist public had thus quite naturally extended their advocacy to encompass the preservation of a broader urban landscape.[10] In St. Petersburg, such initiatives prompted the city's successful application to UNESCO for designation as a "World Cultural Monument."[11] In Yaroslavl, they led to the designation of the city's central districts as a "preservation zone."[12]

The Yaroslavl preservation zone is the result of a decade-long struggle involving mobilized citizen groups, professional architectural organizations, and entrenched planning bureaucrats. The Regional Executive Committee approved the Yaroslavl Preservation Zone Decree only in June 1990, nearly fifteen years after it had first been proposed. That decree established three different types of preservation zones within the Yaroslavl Region.[13] First, construction was prohibited in areas of particular historic value, such as the center city in Yaroslavl. Second, new

[9]This point was made during a tour of historical sites in the Moscow Region with Dmitrii Shvidkovsky, an architectural historian at the Moscow Architectural Institute, on April 20, 1993.

[10]Interview, Ksenia Sokolova, Member, Architectural Planning Staff, Yaroslavl Regional Executive Committee, Yaroslavl, June 24, 1990; Interview, Viktor Fedorovich Marov, Member, Architectural Planning Staff, Yaroslavl Regional Executive Committee, Yaroslavl, December 13, 1990.

[11]Interview, Nikolashchenko, September 13, 1991; interview, Boris Nikolaevich Ometov, Chairman, St. Petersburg Division of the State Inspectorate for the Preservation of Monuments, St. Petersburg, September 12–13, 1991.

[12]Interview, Vladimir Bogordetskii, Chief Architect, Yaroslavl Regional Executive Committee, and Vladimir Izanov, Deputy Chief, Yaroslavl City Executive Committee Architectural Administration, and Vladimir Bykov, Member, Architectural Planning Staff, Yaroslavl Regional Executive Committee, Yaroslavl, June 22, 1990; interview, Vasil'eva, and Father Mikhail Mikhailovich Peregudov, Deputy, Yaroslavl Regional Soviet, and Pavel Grigorievich Boborykin, Deputy Director, Department of Culture, Yaroslavl Regional Executive Committee, Yaroslavl, June 25, 1990; interview, Marov, December 13, 1990; interview, Bobovich, October 14, 1991.

[13]Interview, Vasil'eva, Peregudov, and Boborykin, June 25, 1990.

construction was permitted in another set of districts only after the completion of extensive review. Third, a number of rural districts were set aside to protect the integrity of landscapes deemed to be of particular value. This last provision won the backing of a powerful regional environmental movement.[14]

The campaign to designate major portions of the city of Yaroslavl as a preservation zone grew out of provisions contained in the 1976 USSR Law on Historic Preservation, as well as enabling regulations issued by the USSR Ministry of Culture a decade later.[15] Procedures set forth by central authorities established the guidelines for the creation of preservation zones. Between 150 and 200 Russian cities were identified at that time as having historic value. Subsequent city plans in those communities were required to contain provisions for preservation initiatives.

Opposition to the preservation zone concept by local Communist Party authorities inhibited preservation planning in Yaroslavl until popular political movements brought the issue forward during the late 1980s. By 1988, preservation activism had become increasingly subsumed—together with the local environmental movement—within a broader anti-Communist coalition that organized itself as the Yaroslavl "People's Front" *(narodnyi front)*. The hostility of the local Communist Party boss, Fyodor Loshchenkov, to historic preservation only fueled confrontation between preservationists and Communist officials.[16]

Meanwhile, a number of professional architects had prepared drawings illustrating how the city might have appeared in the thirteenth, seventeenth, eighteenth, and nineteenth centuries.[17] Their depictions demonstrated the replacement of wooden structures by stone buildings during the seventeenth and eighteenth centuries, as well as the creation of the Catherinian street plan during the latter half of the eighteenth century. Both developments were portrayed as being of particular significance in the emergence of a national Russian urban system.[18]

[14]Interview, Lidia Ivanovna Baikova, Environmental Activist, Yaroslavl, June 22, 1990.
[15]This account of the formulation of the Yaroslavl Preservation Zone Decree is based on interview, Marov, December 13, 1990. Marov is widely regarded as the prime mover and author of the decree.
[16]This discussion is based on correspondence with Yaroslavl historic preservation activist Boris Sergeev (March 29, 1993), who later entered a graduate program in political science at the University of California, Santa Barbara.
[17]Many of these materials are now found in the Museum of the City of Yaroslavl. Interview, Ankudinova, June 25, 1990.
[18]The importance of Yaroslavl within the Russian urban system from the tenth century on is the subject of exciting new scholarship by local historians (interview, Viacheslav Nikolaevich Kozliakov, Professor of History, Yaroslavl State University, Yaroslavl, Decem-

Figure 19. Cathedral of the Transfiguration in the Spaso-Preobrazhenskii (Saviour) Monastery. Photograph by William C. Brumfield.

The work of architects and historians, work based on local archival and bibliographic collections, eventually provided the necessary justification for the creation of preservation zones in the city of Yaroslavl as well as elsewhere in the Yaroslavl Region. The June 1990 decree created a "preserve" *(zapovednik)* within which all new construction is prohibited. The local kremlin—which is actually the Spaso-Preobrazhenskii (Saviour) Monastery (Figure 19)—sits at the center of this zone. The borders of this district generally follow the boulevards constructed along the site of the long-destroyed fortifications that once surrounded central Yaroslavl.

Another area open to restricted construction set out an arc running more or less from the trans-Volga bridge toward the Kotorosl', ending at the stadium-circus complex along Freedom Street. A three-story height limit has been imposed in this second area (Figure 20). The Regional

ber 13, 1990; interview, Evgenii Viktorovich Anisimov, Senior Researcher, Institute of History, Russian Academy of Sciences, St. Petersburg, September 11, 1991; interview, Kozliakov and Sevastianova, October 15, 1991, and April 28, 1992). The city's role in the development of a distinctive Russian architectural style is discussed in Brumfield, *A History of Russian Architecture,* pp. 156–64.

Figure 20. Reconstruction and modernization of a historic house in Preservation Zone Two, Yaroslavl, 1993. Photograph by Blair A. Ruble.

Executive Committee's Preservation Administration, together with the local branch of the All-Russian Society for the Preservation of Monuments, must approve all new construction here as well. A third zone, meandering farther away from the city center, regulates construction of buildings up to five stories. All of these measures were predicated on the continuation of state ownership of buildings and land, so that additional ordinances are now required to effectively regulate private economic activity and construction in these areas.

A LANDMARK COURT BATTLE

Concern over violations of building regulations within the preserve surfaced within the city mini-council when, in February 1992, complaints were brought against organizations that had proceeded with the demolition of structures within the historic city center without the permission of city authorities.[19] The mini-council instructed Mayor Volonchunas to

[19]Malyi sovet Iaroslavskogo gorodskogo soveta narodnykh deputatov, "Reshenie No. 13

work with the city council's standing commissions on ecology and culture and historic preservation to develop viable enforcement mechanisms without delay. By the fall of that year, the "Kovalev Affair" promised to establish future enforcement standards.[20]

In early 1992, a joint German-Russian investment firm—Yarkassel Systems, which had grown out of Yaroslavl's sister-city relations with Kassel, Germany—purchased the Engel'gard House at 33 Respublikanskaia Street. Vladimir Andreevich Kovalev, who had been the last Soviet-era chairman of the Yaroslavl Regional Executive Committee, headed this firm. Kovalev had gained notoriety for lavish (by local standards) sausage-and-beer bashes during his March 1990 electoral campaign. He continued to be regarded by many Yaroslavtsy as the leader of the final remnants of the local Communist Party *nomenklatura* within the city of Yaroslavl.[21] Later, Kovalev and his partners in Yarkassel Systems reputedly lured Mercedes-Benz to open a dealership in town.

The Engel'gard House, an eighteenth-century masonry and wood structure in poor repair, stood well within Yaroslavl's historic preservation zone. Local officials interpreted President Yeltsin's ban on private ownership of "historic monuments" as inoperative in this case because the actual structure in question had not itself been designated as a historic monument but was merely located within a "historic preservation zone." Preservation and planning officials in other Russian cities such as St. Petersburg, it should be pointed out, initially endorsed a broader interpretation of President Yeltsin's decree and sought to protect all structures within preservation districts from destruction or misuse by private owners. By late 1993, however, titles to historic buildings across Russia were being granted to private owners regardless of such legal and administrative prohibitions.[22]

Kovalev and his colleagues tore down the Engel'gard House to make room for a new commercial building (Figure 21). Chief Architect Arkady Bobovich and Regional Preservation Administration Director Tat'iana Vasil'eva protested, but to no avail. Kovalev claimed that, since he had

o zapreshchenii snosa starykh zdanii i sooruzhenii v zonakh okhrany i regulirovanii zastroiki g. Iaroslavlia" (February 5, 1992).

[20] Interview, Bobovich, September 1, 1992; interview, Vasil'eva, September 3, 1992.

[21] For a discussion of Kovalev's political role during the last years of the Soviet regime, see Hahn and Helf, "Old Dogs and New Tricks," pp. 519, 525–26.

[22] Interview, Oleg Harchenko, Chief Architect, St. Petersburg Mayor's Office, Baltimore, Md., October 2, 1992; interview, Ometov, October 2, 1992; interview, Lev Petrovich Tikhonov, Deputy Chair, St. Petersburg Branch of the Russian Society for the Preservation of Monuments, Baltimore, Md., October 2, 1992.

Figure 21. Site of the former Engel'gard House, at 33 Respublikanskaia Street, Yaroslavl, 1993. Photograph by Blair A. Ruble.

purchased the building, it was his property and he could do with it as he pleased. Bobovich and Vasil'eva contended that preservation regulations extended to private property as well as state-owned buildings. They turned to the local procurator's office to initiate criminal proceedings for violation of preservation laws. The procurator observed that the Soviet/Russian court system had never upheld preservation regulations, except for a handful of Soviet-era rulings in Leningrad (St. Petersburg). Despite such early inhibitions, the Yaroslavl procurator initiated a criminal investigation after much prompting by the local news media.

Prosecution of the case was momentarily delayed when, in March 1993, the Yaroslavl Regional Council refused to lift parliamentary immunity for a regional deputy involved in the scandal.[23] Since Yarkassel Systems had received permission to raze the Engel'gard House, the procurator's office concluded, charges must be brought against the official who—in the middle of the night—had signed the requisite demolition permits. The offending official—V. N. Nefedov—turned out to be a po-

[23]Interview, Verbitskii, April 14, 1993; interview, Bobovich, April 15, 1993.

litical protégé of Kovalev's and a member of the regional council. For Procurator Oleg Fisun to proceed to court, he was required to request that the regional council suspend Nefedov's parliamentary immunity. The issue came to a vote in late March 1993, with 70 deputies voting in favor of prosecution and 35 opposed.[24] This tally fell short of the 96 votes—or half of the total regional council membership—required to lift immunity and grant permission to Fisun to continue prosecution of Nefedov. Of the total membership, 36 deputies were absent from the session, another 30 deputies abstained, 12 simply failed to indicate any sort of vote at all, and the remaining seats were vacant.

Kovalev and other more visible figures in the affair successfully fended off prosecution on the grounds that they were not directly involved in the management of the construction crew that had pulled the building down. Although these developments were dispiriting for many involved in the prosecution of the case, charges continued to be developed against three others directly involved in tearing down the Engel'gard House.[25]

The initial trial date of August 27, 1993, was postponed because nearly all of the major witnesses were on vacation. Many local observers concluded that no trial would ever take place.[26] However, a four-day trial in late September 1993 ended with "judicial repudiations" against Yarkassel General Director K. V. Fliagin and the firm's administrative director, V. I. Bulatov.[27] Court testimony revealed that Fliagin had been involved in the destruction of numerous historic buildings—including the Moskva restaurant and the Evropa café—during his tenure as the city's housing administrator in the 1970s. Nefedov's role in the whole affair was similarly excoriated even though prosecutors could not bring formal charges against him. Judge S. V. Rezvikov tired of the defendants' bitter protestations of innocence, thundering out the guilty verdicts before open court. Fliagin and Bulatov were convicted of violating articles 230 and 171 of the Russian Federation Criminal Code concerning the intentional destruction of historic and cultural monuments. Sentenced to eighteen months of corrective labor *(ispravitel'naia rabota)* at their jobs,

[24]"Iz protokola N 65 schetnoi komissii o poimennom golosovanii po voprosu o predstavlenii prokurora oblasti O. A. Fisuna o dache soglasiia na privlechenie k ugolovnoi otvetstvennosti deputata Nefedova, V. N.," *Zolotoe kol'tso,* March 26, 1993, p. 3.

[25]Interview, Bobovich, April 15, 1993, and September 9, 1993; interview, Iurii Vital'evich Belaev, Chief Engineer, Yaroslavl Regional Bureau for the Protection and Restoration of Historical and Cultural Monuments, Yaroslavl, September 9, 1993.

[26]Interview, Rumiantseva, November 10, 1993.

[27]Larisa Fabrichnikova, "Dazhe rzhavogo gvozdiia ne ostavili," *Zolotoe kol'tso,* October 8, 1993, p. 4.

with fines valued at 20 percent of their *state* incomes, Fliagin and Bulatov railed away against local journalists and politicians as they left the courthouse. Claiming that they had been framed by "pro-Yeltsin forces," they swore revenge.

Many in Yaroslavl believe that the outcome of the "Kovalev Affair" will secure historic preservation regulation not just in their city but throughout post-Soviet Russia.[28] At a minimum, Deputy Mayor Vladimir Aleksandrovich Kovalev—no relation to the founder of Yarkassel Systems—has been prompted to propose the establishment of a public fund to support restoration of privatized historic buildings by their new owners.[29] The mayor's office also created the Department for the Reconstruction of Historic Structures in May 1993 to deal with preservation concerns. The department is directed by the irascible City Council Deputy Iurii Verbitskii.[30]

In September 1993, Verbitskii explained the role of his new department primarily as that of an advocate for preservation issues within the city administration.[31] The four researchers on his staff were conducting a complete history of downtown buildings block by block. He hoped that they would also develop plans and proposals for others to implement. In addition, the department sought to produce inventories of historic sites to assist municipal and private developers with planning in the future.

Verbitskii reported directly to the deputy mayor's office and operated with core support from the city budget.[32] The department earned additional income by providing certificates to the owners of historic sites for a fee (the first such certificate went to the local pedagogical university). He was trying to participate in all internal municipal discussions touching on historic sites, proposing but not imposing standards. Verbitskii's office, then, was essentially the institutionalization from within the local

---

[28]Interview, Bobovich, September 1, 1992, April 15, 1993, and September 9, 1993; interview, Vasil'eva, September 3, 1992; interview, Belaev, September 9, 1993.
[29]"Eshche odin fond . . . ," *Gorodskie novosti,* September 3–9, 1992, p. 2.
[30]Information provided to Jeffrey Hahn of Villanova University on a visit to Yaroslavl in June 1993.
[31]Interview, Verbitskii, September 7, 1993.
[32]Ibid.

government of the popular movement that had successfully advanced the establishment of a preservation zone some three years before.

Several alternative organizational forms have been established in other historic cities to similarly advance preservation initiatives as local officials have supported preservation with an eye toward enhancing municipal revenues. In Novgorod, the local culture department has created a preservation department, and in Rybinsk—an old industrial center in the Yaroslavl Region—the local city council and municipal administrations have organized competing preservation bureaus.[33] Meanwhile, for-profit *(khozraschetnyi)* historic site development agencies have begun operation in nearby Vladimir and Pereslavl-Zalesski.[34] Such agencies demonstrate the growing attention being paid both to revenue enhancement and to preservation concerns. They also demonstrate the extent to which Russian cities are beginning to develop their own local structures, institutions, and solutions to community concerns. The post-Soviet decline of central authority has created the political and bureaucratic space within which communities can act on their own. Russian governmental organizational charts no longer look exactly alike at the local level.[35]

Verbitskii's new department coexists with a preservation group within the Office of the Chief Architect, as well as with the Regional Administration for the Protection and Restoration of Historical and Cultural Monuments.[36] Jurisdictional lines and divisions of authority and responsibility had yet to be worked out as Verbitskii set out to establish his own bureaucratic domain. Tensions between the development interests of the chief architect, the professionalism of the regional administration, and the populism of the new department undoubtedly will erupt into battles over turf and budgetary allocations. A genuine danger exists that these new arrangements will become so labyrinthine that advocates for preservation concerns will neutralize one another in internecine disputes.

MONEY VERSUS AESTHETICS

Preservation programs in Yaroslavl and elsewhere in Russia that attempt to secure congenial environments have come into conflict with a growing

[33]Ibid.

[34]Ibid.; interview, Vyacheslav Glazychev, President, Moscow Branch, European Academy of the Urban Environment, Moscow, September 4, 1993; Andrei Rybakov, "Sud'ba sobstvennosti, kak sobstvennaia sud'ba," *Vash vybor*, 1993, no. 1 (January): 14–16.

[35]This point was emphasized with pride by Iurii Verbitskii, in Interview, Verbitskii, September 7, 1993.

[36]Ibid.; interview, Belaev, September 9, 1993; interview, Bobovich, September 9, 1993.

demand for locally generated capital.[37] Since 1989, several issues have highlighted the divisions among those sympathetic to preservation of Yaroslavl's built environment now that money has taken on new meaning.

First, proposals by a German hotel firm to build a tourist complex next to the local circus attracted the ire of those who preferred less commercial use of central sites.[38] Proponents pointed to the German firm's proven capacity to operate modern facilities that attract international tourists and their hard currency while preserving the urban landscape. Some opponents of the project remained skeptical of the German firm's specific plans and designs, whereas others were simply opposed to the commercialization of an area of historic significance. In the end, the Germans withdrew their proposal in the wake of the mid-1992 collapse of the Russian economy.[39]

Despite the German withdrawal, a number of other local and foreign proposals for developing tourist facilities within the historic city center remained under consideration at the end of 1993. One locally praised proposal by the French Phoenix construction firm included plans to open an "international quality" hotel-restaurant complex to be built in a "neo-Russian style" overlooking the Kotorosl' River. The complex was intended to serve as a magnet for the tens of thousands of foreigners living in Moscow.[40] Local architects assumed that this joint project, like the prominent "New Holland" Franco-Russian project in St. Petersburg, promised a greater affinity between national approaches to adaptive reuse and historic preservation than did other cross-national joint ventures.[41] Only time will tell how much more successful French construc-

---

[37]This conflict is evident in many Russian cities. See, for example, V. Grigor'ev's description of preservation issues in central St. Petersburg (V. Grigor'ev, "Kruglyi stol 'SP': Zapovednik Peterburgskoi kul'tury," *S.-Peterburgskaia panorama*, 1992, no. 3, pp. 17–19).

[38]Details about the "German hotel" remain difficult to obtain, and little hard information about the project exists. Disagreement over the project was evident in a number of interviews, including the following: Bogordetskii and Bykov, June 22, 1990; Boris Nikolaevich Kuznetsov, Deputy Chair for Culture, Yaroslavl City Executive Committee, Yaroslavl, June 22, 1990; Sokolova, June 24, 1990; Ankudinova, June 25, 1990; Vasil'eva, Peregudov, and Boborykin, June 25, 1990; Marov, December 13, 1990; Bobovich, October 14, 1991; and members of the Yaroslavl Division of the USSR Union of Architects at a meeting hosted by Division Chairman Mesian on October 11, 1991.

[39]Interview, Bobovich, September 1, 1992.

[40]Interview, Kruglikov, April 28, 1992; interview, Bobovich, September 1, 1992; Aleksandr Tsvetkov, "Prikliucheniia frantsuzov v gostinitse 'Kotorosl'," *Zolotoe kol'tso*, October 6, 1993, p. 1.

[41]On the "New Holland" project, see " 'Novaia Golandiia'. Kakoi ei byt?," *S.-Peterburgskaia panorama*, 1992, no. 4, pp. 18–19.

tion and architectural firms will be in Russia than their Finnish, German, Italian, American, Turkish, and Korean competitors.

Private Russian entrepreneurs are also beginning to make their presence felt in the tourist game. Dzhon Mostoslavskii, a musician with the Yaroslavl Philharmonic, rebuilt an eighteenth-century house along the Volga Embankment for use as a house and as a museum of musical instruments (Figure 22).[42] The building, which was constructed on the foundations of a *fligel'* (outbuilding) to a much larger home, failed to win the approval of purists.[43] It is unlike the original building, and it draws on Russian motifs that were never employed in Yaroslavl. This disquietude has prompted city culture authorities to draft new standards for private museums. But the quality of construction of this particular building is so high, and the design so genial, that only the most curmudgeonly preservation advocate appears to be lastingly incensed. For most Yaroslavtsy, such efforts, though small, are encouraging signs that the "new era" may yet prove to have a few beneficial results.[44]

REFINANCING OFFICIAL PRESERVATION PROGRAMS

The tension between aesthetic and commercial prerogatives has emerged in yet another arena as well. Yaroslavl preservation efforts have long been recognized as having maintained the highest quality of craftsmanship and precision. A number of historic buildings—such as the Volkov Theater—provide invaluable cultural facilities that are quite unusual for a provincial center of Yaroslavl's size and stature (Figure 23). The attention to detail that marked the Yaroslavl approach to preservation rested on a solid base of archival and historical research.[45] The local polytechnic institute capitalized on this reputation by initiating a new training program for preservation architecture in 1990.[46] All these activities and programs required government subsidies in order to continue.

On July 1, 1990, for example, the Regional Preservation Administration was transferred to a "cost-accounting" *(khozraschet)* basis, accord-

[42]T. Gorobchenko, "Nakanune otkrytiia," *Severnyi krai,* September 11, 1993, p. 2.

[43]Interview, Belaev, September 9, 1993.

[44]Interview, Verbitskii, April 14, 1993; interview, Bobovich, April 15, 1993.

[45]This view of the local preservation effort is widely shared in Yaroslavl, as well as in Moscow, among interested specialists. Yaroslavl retains extensive documentation of its history, since it remained relatively untouched by war (a major exception being the shelling of the city in 1918 during the Civil War).

[46]Interview, Vasil'eva, Peregudov, and Boborykin, June 25, 1990; interview, Vasil'eva, December 11, 1990.

Figure 22. Museum of Musical Instruments, on the Volga Embankment, 1993. Photograph by Blair A. Ruble.

ing to which revenues must cover expenditures.[47] The administration's budget had grown in nominal terms from R500,000 in 1985 ($275,000 at the time) to more than R4 million in 1990 ($142,857) in response to popular pressure to increase conservation of historic sites. The administration's staff expanded during this period to include eight professional restorers, plus numerous nonprofessionals and volunteers. Suddenly, the administration was forced to cover costs and, hopefully, earn a profit.

The administration's managers initially anticipated generating income from their archaeological activities, especially since recent regulations had required authoritative excavations of building sites in historic areas before the commencement of construction. The sale of reproductions and the profits from a restoration school were similarly viewed as potential money-earners. A cooperative of administration employees actively pursued profit-making ventures as well.

The administration enjoyed some initial entrepreneurial success. The

[47]Interviews, Vasil'eva, Peregudov, and Boborykin, June 25, 1990; Vasil'eva, December 11, 1990.

Figure 23. The Volkov Theater. Photograph by William C. Brumfield.

general collapse of the Russian economy, however, circumscribed these operations. Runaway inflation devalued preservation budgets. Activities that failed to earn their keep—such as the administration's extensive research operations in local archives—were curtailed.

The regional government initiated quarterly budgeting in 1992, with regional authorities transferring R1.8 million ($8,780) during the first quarter of that year to the Preservation Administration and R30 million ($146,341) the next (funding for federally supported projects continued to arrive from Moscow, although with considerable delay).[48] Many workers, facing mounting financial problems of their own, chose not to continue to work unless they were being paid on a regular basis. Once budgeted funding began to flow again on a predictable basis, the administration was unable to lure many of them back. The consequent departure of some of the region's most qualified restoration specialists devastated regional preservation programs. The programs have struggled on, but without sufficient staff and funding to fulfill their missions.

Facing pressure from a reform-minded Russian Federation govern-

[48]Interview, Vasil'eva, September 3, 1992.

ment, regional officials moved in early 1992 to contract out several preservation projects to newly formed private construction companies. In one particularly tragic incident, the inexperienced company that was hired to restore the two-century-old market complex *(gostinyi dvor)* in nearby Rostov-Veliki simply tore down the structure and began to rebuild it from the foundation up, with modern materials.[49] Such experiences prompted many observers to question the wisdom of seeking to support preservation programs on a for-profit basis.[50] Yet, neither the government of the city of Yaroslavl nor the larger regional government had sufficient funding available to sustain the administration's operations at any level above tokenism.

By mid-1993, the regional government had managed to collect enough revenues to begin to honor commitments in the cultural arena (although federal funding for cultural programs had long since ceased to appear in local coffers). Preservation efforts were given special attention, with local administrators coming to view the region's rich cultural heritage as a resource rather than a liability. By the fall of that year, the Regional Preservation Administration employed ten specialists plus a special representative in Rybinsk, as well as in Pereslavl-Zalesski.[51] It should be noted, however, that other cultural and educational institutions were not faring as well in the local budget wars. Most of the region's higher-education establishments were, at that same moment, teetering on the brink of extinction.[52]

CONFRONTATIONS BETWEEN RELIGIOUS AND CULTURAL INSTITUTIONS

The end of the Soviet regime created new opportunities for religious organizations of all denominations to seek return of former houses of worship that had fallen under state control. Many preservation specialists, for their part, have expressed concern over the ability of religious institutions to properly maintain these numerous historic structures.[53]

---

[49]Ibid.

[50]Interview, Verbitskii, October 15, 1991; interview, Vasil'eva, September 3, 1992.

[51]Interview, Belaev, September 9, 1993.

[52]Interview, Mikhail Mizulin, Director, Regional Information and Data Center, Yaroslavl, September 9, 1993.

[53]Also concerned is Ivan Borisovich Purishev, Yaroslavl's award-winning restoration architect and corresponding member of the International Academy of Architects (I. Vaganova, "Bor'ba za pamiatniki byla nachalom politicheskikh strastei," *Zolotoe kol'tso,* August 15, 1992, p. 4).

Vicious battles consequently erupted in Yaroslavl and elsewhere between the Orthodox Church and cultural institutions housed in former religious institutions.[54] There have been some positive outcomes to these struggles. For example, a felicitous merger of a museum facility and a religious facility was negotiated at Moscow's historic Andronikov Monastery, which had served as the Andrei Rublev Central Museum of Ancient Russian Culture and Arts since the late 1950s.[55]

Tensions and suspicions linger as such successful accommodations between cultural and religious leaders prove to be all too rare. The planetarium in the Siberian city of Tomsk, to cite but one example from well beyond the confines of Moscow, was forced during the summer of 1992 to vacate a nineteenth-century Roman Catholic church that was being returned to its original proprietor. Stepan Sulakshin, the local representative of the Russian president in Tomsk (the *"namestnik"*), anguished over this decision.[56] In the end, he was guided by the fact that the buildings had been "stolen by the Bolsheviks" and, further, that today's youth are no longer interested in planetariums. He nonetheless remained concerned that Russia's new leaders were reverting to "Bolshevik methods" in a feverish attempt to compensate for the injustices of the past.

In Yaroslavl, the issue of the return of religious property led to particularly bitter confrontations between preservation officials and representatives of the Russian Orthodox Church.[57] Painful disagreements over the conveyance of the city's largest religious building—the Church of Elijah the Prophet (Figure 24)—to Orthodox authorities illustrate many of the harsh controversies that have come to divide the local preservation movement.[58]

[54]Interviews, Kiril Emil'evich Razlogov, Director, Scientific Research Institute of Culture (Moscow), Moscow, August 25, 1992, and April 17, 1993, Washington, D.C., September 22–24, 1993. Razlogov, whose institute had been housed for many years in a historic building claimed by the Orthodox Church, became the object of vicious personal attack by "patriotic forces" merely because he wanted his institute to remain at its Soviet-era site until he could secure new facilities elsewhere in Moscow (see, for example, S. Turchenko, "Grimasy Armeisko depolizatsii. Porno v trapeznoi," *Sovetskaia Rossiia,* April 6, 1993, p. 4). Razlogov eventually retained a portion of his institute's facilities through a partnership with a major American corporation.

[55]Interview, Oleg Germanovich Ul'ianov, Chief of the Archaeological Sector, Central Museum of Ancient Russian Culture and Arts, Moscow, April 20, 1993.

[56]Interview, Stepan Stepanovich Sulakshin, Representative of the President of the Russian Republic in the Tomsk Region, Washington, D.C., October 8, 1992.

[57]Interview, Vasil'eva, Peregudov, and Boborykin, June 25, 1990; interview, Peregudov, December 13, 1990; interview, Verbitskii, October 15, 1991.

[58]For further discussion, see Brumfield, *A History of Russian Architecture,* pp. 145–47, and Brumfield, *Fragments.*

Figure 24. Church of Elijah the Prophet. Photograph by William C. Brumfield.

The Church of Elijah the Prophet had been a museum for much of the Soviet era. Orthodox officials demanded that this structure, the most prominent and prestigious in the city, be returned to its original purpose and serve as a place of worship. People's Deputy Father Mikhail Mikhailovich Peregudov effectively drew on his standing within the Orthodox Church and his position on the Yaroslavl Regional Council to guide the process of partial transfer of title through to completion in late 1990 and early 1991.[59] Some local cultural notables—such as Yaroslavl Art Museum curator Irina Bolotseva—led a charge against this transfer.[60] Discussions raged in the press, on local television, and in various government and religious commissions and committees all the way up to the most senior governing bodies of the Russian government and the Orthodox Church in Moscow.

Bolotseva's 1990 article appearing in the major local paper of the period, *Severnyi rabochii (Northern Worker)*, established the parameters

---

[59]Interview, Peregudov, December 13, 1990.
[60]Bolotseva's eloquence on the subject is perhaps even more striking in person than in print, as the author discovered during an informal dinner conversation in Yaroslavl on June 24, 1990.

of debate.[61] Acknowledging that there were reasonable grounds for supporting the transfer of title—the structure was built as a house of worship, the Soviet government had abused and irreparably damaged scores of historic buildings, and justice demanded that stolen property be returned to its rightful owner—Bolotseva contrasted the one-thousand-year history of the Russian Orthodox Church with the two hundred-year history of her own institution.

Local gentry and intellectuals had established the Yaroslavl Art Museum in the eighteenth century to protect icons and religious artifacts from abuse by daily worshipers. One of the oldest art museums in Russia, the Yaroslavl collection had demonstrated, according to Bolotseva, a record of considerable accomplishment that should allay any doubts about its dedication to protecting Russia's patrimony for all Russians. The Bolshevik desecration of churches enhanced the cultural significance of those buildings, icons, frescoes, and artifacts—such as the Church of Elijah the Prophet—that had survived under the museum's protection (Figure 25). Finally, she noted, there was as yet no legal basis for returning the property to its previous owner, the Orthodox Church.

A firestorm of controversy ensued.[62] The passionately supercharged issue of the meaning of "Russian-ness" underlay much of this debate. As an undergraduate history student at Yaroslavl State University explained, "The Church of Elijah the Prophet has emotional meaning for all Yaroslavtsy, even if they do not believe in God. The [Orthodox] Church should not be permitted to assert a new ideological monopoly over the meaning of Russia for Russians."[63]

In the end, the conveyance documents for the church stipulated that its maintenance and management were the combined responsibility of the city council, the region's preservation administration, and local prelates.[64] Religious services may not be conducted during the winter, so as to limit the damage to the building's inestimable frescoes by snow, mud, and bulky outergarments (Figures 26 and 27).[65] It was only in 1993—

[61]I. P. Bolotseva, "Il'ya Prorok: sud'ba i vremia," *Severnyi rabochii,* July 25, 1990, p. 3. *Severnyi rabochii* ceased publication following its enthusiastic support of the failed August 1991 putsch, only to return later as *Severnyi krai.*

[62]See, for example, Alla Sevast'ianova, "Nuzhna pravovaia osnova," *Severnyi rabochii,* August 9, 1990, p. 3; L. Karaseva, "Liudi vo chto-to veriat . . . ," *Severnyi rabochii,* August 9, 1990, p. 3.

[63]Comment during seminar with author, Yaroslavl State University Archaeographic Laboratory, April 28, 1992.

[64]Interview, Verbitskii, September 1, 1992; interview, Vasil'eva, September 3, 1992.

[65]Interview, Verbitskii, October 15, 1991.

Figure 25. Polychrome ceramic tiles and frescoes surrounding the main entrance to the Church of Elijah the Prophet. Photograph by William C. Brumfield.

Figure 26. Interior frescoes, Church of Elijah the Prophet. Photograph by William C. Brumfield.

after most property demands by local religious institutions had been resolved—that relations between some more moderate religious officials and their more restrained colleagues among preservation groups began to improve.[66]

A bitter legacy of recrimination remains as local authorities across Russia decide the fates of scores of religious buildings. The task is enormous. There were 1,200 operating churches in Yaroslavl Province (Iaroslavskaia Guberniia) alone in 1912, whereas only 130 remained open to parishioners in 1993.[67] Meanwhile, the powerful and once united Yaroslavl historical preservation movement has become sharply divided and contentious.

The Yaroslavl experience is characteristic of battles that have exploded throughout post-Soviet Russia. In the nearby Moscow Region, for example, a record number of religious buildings were transferred

[66]Ibid., April 14, 1993.
[67]Sergei Safronov, "V kogo veriat Iaroslavtsy," *Vash vybor,* 1993, no. 2: 28–29.

Figure 27. Interior frescoes, Church of Elijah the Prophet. Photograph by William C. Brumfield.

during 1992 to Orthodox Church authorities.[68] The region, which is an oblast surrounding, but not including, the city of Moscow, has benefited disproportionately from the unleashing of private investment in land and construction that began just a few years ago. The Moscow Region is also the site of some of the oldest and most cherished historic monuments in all of Russia.

St. Petersburg religious leaders and cultural authorities battled well into 1993 over the status of that city's major cathedral, St. Isaac's, which defines the local skyline. Local government officials remained categorically opposed to the transfer of St. Isaac's to the Orthodox Church on the grounds that it served a larger community as a museum. The Russian Federation's Ministry of Culture at the national level officially endorsed such a transfer, thereby linking an already emotion-wrought dispute to the ever explosive question of local autonomy.[69]

[68]Nikolai Olenik, "Problema peredachi khramov ne imeet prostykh reshenii," *Nezavisimaia gazeta*, January 6, 1993, p. 5.
[69]IA 'Severo-Zapad', "Muzhiki ne ishchut kompromissa," *Nezavisimaia gazeta*, January 30, 1993, p. 6.

Russian Federation legislation eventually established clear guidelines for title transfer to religious organizations.[70] Any community of at least twenty believers may register with the Ministry of Justice and file a request before the regional committee on culture and tourism for the free transfer of title to a religious building. Officials of the Moscow Patriarchate may support such a request in those instances involving groups of Orthodox believers. The process usually proceeds without difficulty unless the structure in question has served as a cultural facility (e.g., a library, club, or museum). In such instances, local authorities frequently receive a large number of protests from the general citizenry. In the Moscow Region, officials now seek to guarantee that the Orthodox Church will provide a suitable substitute facility for community institutions. Nonetheless, a backlog of disputed properties involving particularly visible cultural monuments and museums has touched off bitter recriminations and prolonged battles involving local religious and government officials and citizens' groups, as well as representatives of the Moscow Patriarchate.

Museum and religious officials began to tangle over the fate of religious artifacts as many disputes over the disposition of real property were being resolved. Writing in *Vash vybor,* a new national journal devoted to regional affairs, Yaroslavl Art Museum curator Irina Bolotseva once again sounded the alarm.[71] Bolotseva protested plans to empty out icons from the Yaroslavl Art Museum for use in churches around the region. She acknowledged that many icons from the thirteenth through nineteenth centuries came to the museum through state confiscation programs during the 1920s and 1930s—and, most actively, in 1928. The museum had saved hundreds of precious paintings and frescoes from destruction. Although they were not stored in ideal conditions, she continued, they nonetheless received professional care. The Orthodox Church could not similarly protect the hundreds of icons that were scheduled for transfer, at least in the short term. Bolotseva also expressed concern over a newly formed commission that had been established by the regional authorities to supervise the transfer of artifacts from the Yaroslavl Art Museum to the Orthodox Church. She expressed particular skepticism about the competence of some of the region's political figures involved in the process. Once again, Bolotseva was careful not

---

[70]"Zakon RF o svobode veroispovedanii" and "Zakon RSFSR ob okhrane i ispol'zovanii pamiatnikov istorii i kul'tury ot 1978-ogo goda."
[71]I. P. Bolotseva, "Ch'i na rusi ikony?" *Vash vybor,* 1993, no. 1 (January), p. 43.

to deny the legitimacy of the claims of the Orthodox Church. Rather, she enunciated a cautionary note against rushing the transfer of artifacts before the transfer could be properly handled.

WHO OVERSEES THE RUSSIAN PAST?

An even more divisive and emotional quarrel has begun to form around the future of Moscow's Red Square. This battle highlights the extent to which the issues swirling around historic preservation are becoming a focal point for conflicting images of Russia's past and future.

The restorers and architects based at Moscow's Izmailovo Restoration Center have proposed a rather controversial plan for the redevelopment of Russia's best-known urban space.[72] According to this vision, Red Square would become an "iconostasis of the Russian Apocalypse," with an Orthodox cross standing atop the Lenin mausoleum, a Latin cross on *lobnoe mesto* (place of execution) to mark the execution there of martyrs, and seven reconstructed chapels that stood on the square "before Peter removed them in a fit of Europeanization." Other, more secular features of the ensemble would include a tower sporting a statue of St. George slaying the dragon (as in Moscow's official seal), the Minin and Pozharskii Monument relocated near its original spot in front of what is now GUM, and near the river, a trading area that would be supported by "Azerbaidzhani and Armenian bankers." This plan combined Orthodoxy and Russian nationality, an integration that is offensive to less religious Russians. It also threatened the use of the square, in the wake of communism's collapse, for public entertainment (including rock concerts).

Divisions are similarly apparent in St. Petersburg, with a more local accent. Many survivors of the German-Finnish siege of the city from late 1941 until January 1944 opposed the renaming of the city from Leningrad back to the original St. Petersburg. For veterans of the Second World War, the name "Leningrad" carried an emotional impact quite independent from its connection with the founder of the Soviet state. Beyond emotions, proponents of "Leningrad" wondered precisely what sort of traditional "Petersburgers" contemporary residents of the city

---

[72]Interview, Viktor Vinogradov, Chief Architect, Izmailovo Restoration Center (Moscow), Moscow, August 28, 1992.

could become.[73] Put somewhat differently, which "Petersburg" heritage would be preserved? The aristocratic city of the turn of the nineteenth century, the industrial city of the turn of the twentieth, or some other "Petersburg"? Answers to that question are emotionally and ideologically charged. Conflict is inevitable and, most likely, irresolvable.

Yaroslavl city authorities have stumbled into similar quarrels over street names. In this instance, officials opted to publicize various previous names rather than designating one to be the most politically correct (Figure 28). More troubling for confirmed Petersburgers and Yaroslavtsy alike, it seems, was the absence of orderly mechanisms for determining winners and losers in these confrontations over core beliefs.[74] Once again, preservation in the post-Soviet era had become intertwined with contending images of the nation, thereby tearing apart preservation alliances that had once mobilized thousands of citizens in confrontation with Communist power. The complexity of Russia's new urban realities undermined the viability of one of the country's most animated grassroots political movements.

In his distinguished review of the uses and misuses of history, *The Past Is a Foreign Country,* David Lowenthal observed, "However faithfully we preserve, however authentically we restore, however deeply we immerse ourselves in bygone times, life back then was based on ways of being and believing incommensurable with our own."[75] The past, Lowenthal continues, is celebrated "through present-day lenses." Yet, the use of the past is critical for understanding the present. Stefan Tanaka, writing about Japan, concluded, "The past not only gives us identity, but in doing so also renders the unfamiliar into an understandable order, reaffirms and preserves parts of ourselves, and provides guidance."[76] It is just such guidance that Russians seek as they attempt to piece their nation and their identity back together following the cataclysm of the Soviet era.

In a Russia searching for new lenses, differing views of the present and hopes for the future naturally sustain differing views of the past. Similar quarrels occur, of course, in many historic towns and cities

---

[73]Vladimir Lisovskii, "Spasti i sokhranit'," *S.-Peterburgskaia panorama,* 1992, no. 4, pp. 28–30.

[74]Interview, Ometov, October 2, 1992; interview, Tikhonov, October 2, 1992.

[75]David Lowenthal, *The Past Is a Foreign Country* (Cambridge: Cambridge University Press, 1985), p. xvi.

[76]Stefan Tanaka, *Japan's Orient: Rendering Pasts into History* (Berkeley: University of California Press, 1993), p. 266.

Figure 28. A Yaroslavl street has many names. Photograph by Blair A. Ruble.

around the world. The problem of the moment in Yaroslavl is to establish mechanisms that will facilitate their constructive resolution. The degree of openness permitted by the procedures that eventually emerge will partially determine how urban space will be reinvented in Yaroslavl's post-Soviet future.

4

Replanning Yaroslavl

To this point, this study has focused on policy issues that derive from the decisions and actions of individual institutions and people. The decision to privatize an apartment is quite personal; a state agency's effort to develop special housing for pensioners, in the same vein, involves specific sites and small groups of people. Construction of single-family homes and battles over the preservation of historic buildings, though more sweeping in character, similarly involve specific building lots and neighborhoods. Such largely individualized—or at least compartmentalized—decisions eventually fit into a larger urban fabric. The weave of that fabric has itself changed in post-Soviet Yaroslavl as money has come to take on added significance.

The Soviet city-planning effort was rigidly bureaucratized and enigmatic when it confronted individual choice. Frustration with overcentralized planning procedures prompted local revolt against national planning agencies at the very first sign of perestroika-era reform. Since that time, planners and politicians have grappled with new city-building phenomena driven by market forces. This chapter examines that struggle.

Land-use planning on the scale of an urban region is not new to a Russian city such as Yaroslavl. Formal plans have existed for decades. Land-use decisions, economic-development strategies, and infrastructure construction were intended to satisfy the needs of enterprises tied to central ministries. The new planning philosophies that have come to the fore over the past half decade incorporate greater concern for environmental quality, aesthetic norms, and individual choice. Yaroslavtsy are reimagining their community and region, and municipal and regional

104

planning agencies are replanning their town. The individual and institutional decisions discussed thus far are being placed into a broader
pattern of urban development. This chapter will examine Soviet-era
plans for Yaroslavl, the gradual departure from those plans since the
mid-1980s, attempts to integrate public participation into the planning
process, and finally, efforts to create a fresh planning strategy for the
post-Soviet 1990s.

SOVIET CITY PLANNING

Before the late 1980s, Soviet cities developed within the parameters of
general plans that expanded over time from an initial focus on physical
development to an incorporation of economic and social factors.[1] These
planning documents, which became the primary instrument for urban
planning, were accompanied by detailed thematic and district projections. The plans elaborated the broad outline of future construction in
a city for a period of up to thirty years. Soviet law required every city
to adopt and implement such a general plan, and many did so, with
varying degrees of practical result. During the period 1945–77, general
plans completed in the Russian S.F.S.R. alone totaled 720, of which 370
were fundamentally revised more than once.[2]

The preparation of a general development plan was a mammoth and
complex undertaking made all the more intricate by the classified nature
of the process. On the one hand, planners were driven to incorporate as
much of urban—indeed, human—existence as possible within their formulas and maps. On the other hand, the extensive economic, demographic, and social informational base that exists in every major city of
the industrialized world was either sealed from view or nonexistent in
the Soviet case. The secretive nature of urban planning preempted constructive dialogue with the community at large.

The entire process was further complicated by the fact that the actual

---

[1] For further discussion of the history of the Soviet general planning process, see Ilya N.
Zaslavsky, "Population Geography and Settlement Planning in the USSR," *Planning Theory Newsletter* (Milano), nos. 5–6 (1991): 179–87, and Bater, *The Soviet City.* On the
incorporation of social variables into physical planning, see Blair A. Ruble, "Policy Innovation and the Soviet Political Process: The Case of Socio-Economic Planning in Leningrad," *Canadian Slavonic Papers* 24, no. 2 (June 1982): 161–74, and Ruble, *Leningrad,*
pp. 155–76.
[2] M. N. Mezhevich, "Upravlenie razvitiem gorodov: potrebnosti i real'nosti," in P. N. Lebedev and V. S. Sukhin, eds., *Chelovek i obshchestvo no. 16: Sotsial'nye problemy planirovaniia sotsialisticheskogo goroda* (Leningrad: LGU-NIIKSI, 1977), pp. 54–55.

preparation of a local general plan was financed by national authorities and carried out by enormous planning institutes in Moscow, Leningrad, and the capital cities of the union republics. As a consequence, the authors of the plans were more often than not only minimally aware of local realities.[3] Many local officials, for their part, simply ignored the plans, since they had largely been left out of the preparation process. In short, urban planning at the end of the Brezhnev era worked about as well as any other form of planning in the Soviet Union.

Despite an explicit preoccupation with the physical development of a city, Soviet general plans rested first and foremost on a region's long-range economic outlook. Economic objectives were set forth in an unpublished document, the "technical-economic foundations" (*tekhniko-ekonomicheskie osnovy* [TEO]) of the future planning project. Architects and physical planners next formulated a detailed strategy to transform these economic objectives into construction and architectural design programs. Their efforts prepared the way for the formulation of the general plan itself. A city's general plan would then be approved by municipal and regional Communist Party and governmental committees and councils before formally being accorded the status of law. Once ratified, general plans were intended to guide a city's development for the next twenty-five to thirty years.[4]

Actual plans were frequently flawed—a phenomenon not unknown outside the Soviet Union. Assumptions about population growth and economic projections often proved false, a pattern familiar to planners everywhere. The consequences of such miscalculation were particularly severe in the Soviet context, since few market mechanisms existed to adjust the miscues of planners and bureaucrats. The 3.5 million "optimal" population ceiling projected in the Leningrad General Plan of 1966, for example, had been breached even before the plan was fully approved in Moscow.[5] Leningrad continued to attract new residents,

[3]This point is developed in Vyacheslav Glazychev's perceptive article "Malyi gorod. Tekhnologiia vyzyvaniia i razvitiia," *Svobodnaia mysl'*, 1993, no. 7, pp. 9–18.

[4]This discussion is based on interview, Nikolai Agafonov, Senior Researcher, Institute of Socio-Economic Problems, USSR Academy of Sciences, Leningrad, February 20, 1984.

[5]"Postanovlenie Soveta Ministrov SSSR o general'nom plane razvitiia g. Leningrada," *Sbornik postanovlenii pravitel'stva SSSR*, 1966, no. 14, pp. 275–82; "General'nyi plan razvitiia Leningrada," in Planovaia komissiia ispolkoma Lengorsoveta, Statisticheskoe upravlenie goroda Leningrada, *Leningrad za 50 let: Statisticheskii sbornik* (Leningrad: Lenizdat, 1967), pp. 163–67; V. A. Kamenskii, *Leningrad. General'nyi plan razvitiia goroda* (Leningrad: Lenizdat, 1972); V. A. Kamenskii, "Itogi desiatiletnego perioda realizatsii general'nogo plana razvitiia Leningrada utverzhennogo Soveta Ministrov SSSR v iiule 1966 goda," *Stroitel'stvo i arkhitektura Leningrada*, 1966, no. 7, pp. 1–47. For an

growing by nearly 1.5 million residents in the next two decades.[6] As a result, all housing, transportation, and service strategies advanced by Leningrad planners in 1966 were immediately obsolete—with virtually no private-sector services to fill the gap left by inadequate public services and construction programs.

The social, economic, and political forces unleashed by perestroika magnified the traditional inadequacies of the Soviet approach to city planning. Whatever the shortcomings of the old system, informal bureaucratic mechanisms had evolved over the years to keep Soviet cities functioning. In Yaroslavl, for example, the massive Avtodizel' Motor Works opened schools, hospitals, and rest homes while constructing some thirty-five thousand apartments for its workers, largely with ministerial funds from Moscow that never passed through city coffers—or city control.[7] These direct expenditures were above and beyond whatever taxes the plant may have paid to local authorities. Employing one-tenth of the city's entire work force (and having some connection with one in five Yaroslavtsy), Avtodizel' arguably exerted greater influence over the shape of the Yaroslavl cityscape during its seventy-five-year history than did local planning officials. As the Soviet Union's primary producer of car, truck, bus, and tank engines, Avtodizel' remained beyond the reach of Yaroslavl planners and elected officers.

The new political and economic realities of the late 1980s subverted the mechanisms by which a plant such as Avtodizel' fashioned a community. With production plummeting (by some 25 to 30 percent at Avtodizel' during 1991 alone), new rules of the game were slow to take shape during the disarray of Gorbachev-era power politics.

PERESTROIKA RECASTS CITY PLANNING

The policies of political openness supported by Mikhail Gorbachev's perestroika campaign encouraged greater transparency in the city planning process. More information was made available to more citizens than ever before (previously, general plans were classified documents). Many municipalities provided more opportunities for citizen involve-

English-language analysis of the 1966 Leningrad General Plan and its aftermath, see Ruble, *Leningrad*, pp. 72–112.

[6]*Narodnoe khoziaistvo Leningrada i Leningradskoi oblasti v desiatoi piatiletke: Statisticheskii sbornik* (Leningrad: Lenizdat, 1981), pp. 23–24.

[7]Interview, Zheltyakov and Chervnikov, April 29, 1992.

ment in planning decisions through public hearings and other partici-
patory forums.

A planners' nightmare followed as their decisions were subject to sec-
ond-guessing from both above and below. In Moscow, for example,
efforts to initiate the preparation of a new general plan for the national
capital were stymied on the one hand when Mikhail Gorbachev and
Stanislav Shatalin attacked the proposal as incompatible with economic
reform.[8] On the other hand, a population emboldened by robust election
campaigns simultaneously began to attack the city planning process as
undemocratic.[9] Russian urbanites, it seems, had come to believe that
noxious facilities should not be built in their neighborhoods, no matter
how necessary the plants might be for the common good. The widely
recognized American phenomenon of "not in my backyard," or
"NIMBY," spread throughout Russian cities as "not in my courtyard"
(ne v moem dvore).

There was every reason for concern among Russian city dwellers;
environmental degradation throughout the former Soviet Union reached
unfathomable levels.[10] Yaroslavl, for its part, ranked among the 99 most
polluted cities in Russia in 1989.[11] A report on soil conditions prepared
during the autumn of 1991 for Yaroslavl city officials concluded, "The
general condition of soil resources in the city of Yaroslavl and its surrounding area is inauspicious *[neblagopriiatnyi]* for human habitation."[12] Overall, the report continued, the Yaroslavl area had
experienced "very high levels of soil polluted with heavy metals," which
made much of the region "undesirable" *(nezhelatel'no)* for agricultural
production. The authors of the report added that the soil and vegetation
of many areas both in the city and in the surrounding region contained

---

[8]Interview, Aleksandr Viktorovich Kuzmichev, Architect, Moscow General Planning Office, Moscow, June 14, 1990.

[9]Ibid.

[10]See, for example, Murray Feshbach and Alfred Friendly, Jr., *Ecocide in the USSR* (New
York: Basic Books, 1992); Peterson, *Troubled Lands;* and B. I. Kochurov, "Rossiia vo
mgle. Ekologicheskii kommentarii," *Vash vybor,* 1993, no. 2 (February), pp. 42–43.

[11]Gosudarstvennyi doklad, "Sostoianie prirodnoi sredy i prirodookhranaia: deiatel'nost' v
SSSR v 1989 gody," as reported in Ruben A. Mnatsakanian, *Environmental Legacy of
the Former Soviet Republics (as Collated from Official Statistics)* (Edinburgh: Centre for
Human Ecology, University of Edinburgh, 1992), p. 136.

[12]Malyi sovet Iaroslavskogo gorodskogo soveta narodnykh deputatov, "Reshenie No. 5 o
meropriiatiiakh po uluchsheniiu ekologicheskogo sostoianiia pochv g. Iaroslavlia i prigorodnykh territorii" (January 23, 1992), and its accompanying "Spravka ob ekologicheskom sostoianii pochv g. Iaroslavlia i prigorodnykh territorii" (submitted to the
Yaroslavl City Soviet Permanent Commission on Ecology on November 26, 1991).

metal levels well above the maximum norm for healthy human habitation. This pollution had damaged the health and lowered the life expectancy of Yaroslavl residents. Shocked by these findings, the newly formed mini-council lent its support to efforts to map soil conditions, reduce chemical and radiation pollution, and integrate environmental data into municipal planning procedures for future land-use and settlement patterns. Nonetheless, an asbestos factory located in the very center of town—one of the major local environmental miscreants—was still hard at work in September 1992.[13] Discovery of a problem did not necessarily lead to its solution.

Economic reform lurched forward throughout the last years of the Soviet period, thereby eroding the powers of state planners.[14] Municipal officials and planners inexperienced in the ways of the market were daunted by the need to incorporate a growing private sector into their economic calculations and forecasts.[15] Manipulation of land rents, taxes, and prices offered more efficient planning mechanisms in an environment in which money and profit were gaining newfound meaning. Interestingly, it was precisely at this moment that preparation of a new general development plan began in the city of Yaroslavl.

A NEW PLAN FOR YAROSLAVL

The Yaroslavl general plan developed in the late 1960s and implemented in the early 1970s sought to separate residential and industrial districts by moving housing to the north (Bragino) and east (Zavolzhskii) of the historic city center.[16] These efforts encouraged the construction of gigantic neighborhoods that housed Yaroslavtsy in enormous, prefabricated "super blocks," or *mikroraiony*.[17] Somewhere near one-half of the city's population came to live in these new districts, inhabiting apartments that were—despite centrally imposed construction norms and floor plans—among the most spacious in the Russian Republic. By the early 1980s, Communist Party authorities claimed, Yaroslavtsy enjoyed

---

[13]Interview, Guseev, September 2, 1992.
[14]Interview, Druzhinin, April 23, 1991, and May 16, 1991.
[15]Interview, Bobovich, October 14, 1991.
[16]Iu. Sdobnov, E. Rozhanov, and A. Ikonnikov, "Iaroslavl'. Tri tochki zreniia na problemu svoeobraziia," *Arkhitektura SSSR,* 1981, no. 9, pp. 16–21.
[17]For further discussion of this pattern of Soviet residential development, see Ruble, "From *Khrushcheby* to *Korobki.*"

the highest per capita allocation of living space in the Russian S.F.S.R. (a boast vigorously disputed by anti-Communist activists).[18]

The general plan of the 1970s failed to adequately address issues of industrial location.[19] The city's oldest and largest industrial enterprises remained in a belt surrounding the city center, especially on the near north side, where heavy industrial plants continued to hum along as they had since the 1930s and before. Housing leapt over the industrial near north side to the Bragino area.

As a result of the inability of local officials to force industry to move, residents suffered from the ill effects of air pollution both in the traditional city center and in the newly built areas. Bragino was linked to the center by inadequate bus and tram lines, necessitating long, uncomfortable, and inconvenient trips to town. Telephone service—together with cable television—reached many buildings only in 1992. Typical Soviet-era development of the new district's service infrastructure demanded that residents repeat their daily commute on off-work days merely to secure food and other goods. These problems might have been alleviated had municipal authorities encouraged factories to relocate to the city's periphery, vacating their current sites for residential and service facilities.

Massive new districts across the Volga to the east similarly remain isolated from downtown. The movement of the city's population to the periphery bled much of the vitality from more traditional neighborhoods both in the city center and across the Kotorosl' River in the Krasnoper-ekopskii District. Recalling his boyhood, Regional Council Deputy Gennadi Ol'khovik lamented the construction of massive *korobki* (boxes), which are, he remarked, "nothing more than high-rise *baraki* (barracks)." Ol'khovik claimed that the "vibrant street life of single-story life" had been lost (Figure 29).[20]

The very success in the implementation of the planners' vision for the

---

[18]Interview, Viktor Maksimovich Barabash, Retired First Secretary of the Yaroslavl City Communist Party Committee and Secretary for Construction of the Yaroslavl Regional Communist Party Committee, Yaroslavl, June 26, 1990.

[19]These observations are based on a series of discussions with Yaroslavl residents, including planners and architects, as well as excursions around the city in June 1990, December 1990, October 1991, April 1992, September 1992, and April 1993. Group discussions were also held in Yaroslavl with Bogordetskii, Izanov, and Bykov, June 22, 1990; with members of the Yaroslavl Division of the USSR Union of Architects hosted by Division Chairman Mesian on October 11, 1991; and a joint Russian-American conference on problems of local governance convened in Yaroslavl on April 27–28, 1992.

[20]Interview, Gennadi Feodos'evich Ol'khovik, Chair, Commission on Science, Education, Culture, and Upbringing of the Yaroslavl Regional Council of People's Deputies, Yaroslavl, April 14, 1993.

Figure 29. Church of St. Nicholas the Wet, Yaroslavl. Photograph by William C. Brumfield.

future of Yaroslavl had the unintended effect of fragmenting a once unified urban community. As noted earlier, six separate population centers have formed within the city's planning boundaries, each manifesting distinct social and economic characteristics. These quite discrete settlements stretch out for nearly fifty miles along the banks of the Volga. The boundaries among the city's administrative districts have become more pronounced with the results of 1970s policies that sought to intensify the segregation of the city by function.

As in other Soviet cities, the intentions of planners were implemented in Yaroslavl through administrative means and bureaucratic bargaining.[21] Major enterprises were subordinated directly to either union-republic or all-union ministries, even as local soviets attempted to be the "masters of their own cities" *(khoziain goroda)*. Less important enterprises remained subordinate to regional or city officials. Municipal obligations multiplied to encompass previously private economic activities, with every economic unit from factory shop to urban district to industrial ministry becoming locked into a single hierarchical system dominated by an overarching network of Communist Party committees. Planners in Yaroslavl and elsewhere translated their plans into reality by learning to navigate within this system. Constructing new housing on previously vacant land, to cite but one example, proved to be much easier than forcing the relocation of enterprises supported by entrenched ministries in Moscow. Such construction strategies are driven by cost considerations in the West. Under Soviet conditions, a similar physical result—the construction of large housing complexes on vacant land— was a consequence of bureaucratic expediency or the prudent calculation of political rather than economic cost.

CITY PLANNING IS DECENTRALIZED

The rules of urban management changed substantially during the late 1980s.[22] The reach of major central construction and design agencies in Moscow—such as the USSR State Committee on Construction (Gosstroi) and the USSR Union of Architects—began to be curtailed in 1987. A joint resolution by the Communist Party's Central Committee and the

[21]These activities are described in greater detail in Ruble, *Leningrad,* pp. 7–15, 193–220.
[22]This section is based on interview, Bogordetskii, Izanov, and Bykov, June 22, 1990, as well as on a discussion by members of the Yaroslavl Division of the USSR Union of Architects hosted by Division Chairman Mesian on October 11, 1991.

USSR Council of Ministers in August of that year fostered five major innovations in urban planning processes. First, central design standards were rescinded so that regions and their principal cities such as Yaroslavl could bring planning and design standards into conformity with local conditions and preferences. Second, the resolution proposed that Gosstroi be divided into competing regional construction authorities. Third, the Central Committee and Council of Ministers recommended the accompanying replacement of the state construction materials monopoly by regional administrations. Fourth, the education of architects and others involved in the construction process was to be decentralized beginning in 1989. Fifth, the rights and powers of municipal agencies over local construction and urban planning processes were extended to encompass qualitative as well as quantitative indices.

Local authorities across Russia gained unprecedented control over local urban planning decisions as a consequence of these decisions as well as the more general disintegration of central authority. New land-use regulations and taxes approved by the Russian Federation Parliament in 1991 promised local officials even more powerful levers for limiting land consumption by industrial enterprises.[23] Russian Federation laws that would have permitted foreign ownership of nonagricultural land, legislation initially proposed in June 1992, would have further altered land-use patterns had they been implemented and enforced.[24] Mechanisms of land-use management will change further as economic and political decentralization continues.

In March 1992, Yaroslavl officials seized the opportunities being created by the Russian Federation government for local initiative to reimagine the physical form of their city. They sponsored an inventory of land-use patterns and established a new system of land-use tax rates as a first step toward reinventing land-use patterns.[25] Initial tax rates ranged between R3.71 and R7.77 (between $.03 and $.06 at the time) per square meter of land occupied by enterprises and between R.11 and

[23]Interview, Iurii Bocharov, Chairman, Soviet Society of Urbanists, Washington, D.C., March 22, 1991, and May 9, 1991; interview, Nikolashchenko, September 13, 1991; interview, Valentina Vladimirovna Istomina, Chief, Financial-Budget Department, Yaroslavl City Executive Committee, Yaroslavl, October 11, 1991; interview, Bobovich, October 14, 1991; interview, Polunin, October 17, 1991; interview, Kaganova and Maslennikov, October 22, 1991; interview, Fadeev, December 12, 1991.
[24]Hiatt, "Yeltsin to Let Foreigners Buy Russian Land."
[25]Malyi sovet Iaroslavskogo gorodskogo soveta narodnykh deputatov, "Reshenie No. 41 o provedenii inventarizatsii zemli i stroenii i utverzhdenii stavok zemel'nogo naloga na territorii g. Iaroslavlia" (March 18, 1992).

R.23 (R1 = $.008) per square meter of land with houses and dachas—
or cottages—occupied by individuals. These charges were accompanied
by fines ranging from a low of R50 for organizations and R1 for individuals (between $.41 and $.008) illegally occupying building sites to
R1 million for organizations and R5,000 for individuals (between
$8,000 and $50) destroying valuable subsoils through pollution or in-
appropriate land use.[26]

Yaroslavl planning officials continue to struggle to devise for their
city new development strategies that will direct economic growth within
the context of hyperinflation, a privatizing economy, and political uncertainty. Deputy Mayor Vladimir Aleksandrovich Kovalev has complained bitterly about the impossibility of planning for future
development in a period of social and economic breakdown.[27] City officials shelved projections of housing demand in late 1992, for example,
as they scrambled to accommodate a stream of refugees from ethnic
warfare in the Caucasus.[28] The consequent ethnic tensions—a large pro-
portion of the refugees were not Russian—and the accompanying drain
on already overextended municipal resources tempered any notion that
urban development could be planned or that a community could be
reinvented from above.[29]

City leaders attempted to plan for their city's future as best they
could. In higher education, they moved to consolidate a number of small
and ineffectual institutions of higher education into a single, regional
"federal university."[30] As for fiscal concerns, Beth Mitchneck reports
that Yaroslavl officials proved themselves to be surprisingly effective in
sustaining revenue flows—increasing total budgetary revenues nineteen-
fold between 1991 and 1992 (an achievement considerably diminished
by inflation).[31] Local tax collectors expanded revenues from the profit

[26]Malyi sovet Iaroslavskogo gorodskogo soveta narodnykh deputatov, "Reshenie No. 12
   o poriadke osushchestvleniia kontrolia za ispol'zovaniem i okhranoi zemel' v g. Iaroslavle" (January 23, 1992).
[27]Interview, Vladimir Aleksandrovich Kovalev, First Deputy Mayor, Yaroslavl City, Yaroslavl, September 4, 1992.
[28]For a brief analysis of refugee migration to the Yaroslavl region, see Irina Pavlova,
   "Strannopriimnyi dom na Rostovskom trakte," *Vash vybor,* 1993, no. 1 (January), pp.
   22–23.
[29]Concern over ethnic conflicts prompted local officials to convene a national conference
   in January 1993 bringing together specialists on ethnic relations from around Russia
   (Interview, Rumiantseva, April 16, 1993, and interview, Mizulin, April 16, 1993).
[30]"V oblastnoi administratsii," p. 1.
[31]Beth Mitchneck, "The Changing Role of the Local Budget in Russian Cities: The Case
   of Yaroslavl'," in Hahn and Friedgut, *Local Power and Post-Soviet Politics,* and Beth

tax on local enterprises and from individual income taxes and exploited new sources of revenues tied to privatization and usage fees. Most important, the city developed an integrated revenue and budgetary system for the first time. Mitchneck concludes that Yaroslavl financial officials grasped the implications of post-Soviet fiscal decentralization and became activists "attempting to produce a new system, not to reproduce the previous system."[32] This accomplishment, which was remarkable given the disruptions of the period, largely parallels patterns in physical urban planning.

A PLAN FOR THE 1990S

Turning to physical planning, the Yaroslavl City Executive Committee engaged the services of the Central Scientific Research and Design Institute for City Construction in 1990 to prepare a new citywide general development plan.[33] According to the joint agreement of the local executive committee with the Moscow-based institute, the two parties would seek to formulate the new "social-production and legal-ecological basis" for a new general plan before the end of 1993. Planners were asked to view the city and a region within fifty kilometers of its planning boundaries as a single, integrated region. Several alternative projections of future development were to be proposed, with greater flexibility expected in plan implementation than in the past. Traditional concerns for cultural, economic, social, and physical development would be joined with a greater emphasis on ecological issues. Local officials sought expanded authority over monitoring and directing urban development. Some politicians encouraged expanded community participation in the planning process. The veil of secrecy that has obscured planning decisions would be lifted.[34]

By late 1992, the planning team agreed to develop a number of al-

Mitchneck, "The Local Budget in the Changing Role of Municipal Government in Russia: A Case Study of Iaroslavl'," *Report of the National Council for Soviet and East European Research,* 1993.

[32]Mitchneck, "The Local Budget in the Changing Role of Municipal Government in Russia," p. 17.

[33]Malyi sovet Iaroslavskogo gorodskogo soveta narodnykh deputatov, "Programma-Zadanie na razrabotku general'nogo plana g. Iaroslavlia, utverzhdenno Predsedatel'em ispolkoma Iaroslavskogo gorodskogo soveta narodnykh deputatov i TsNIIP gradostritel'stva" (Iaroslavl', 1990).

[34]Given the extensive literature on the planning process in other societies, this newfound openness in Russia expands the possibilities for genuinely comparative scholarship on the nature of urban planning in a variety of social, economic, and political environments.

ternative plans that would be presented for public discussion within approximately one year.[35] The city's elected agencies would consider these competing concepts for the future of Yaroslavl, presenting them to the public for discussion. Once general objectives had been established, elected officials would turn the planning process back to the professionals for elaboration. The entire process was to be completed before the end of 1994.

In March 1993, the Moscow-based consultants reported to Yaroslavl municipal authorities, proposing three radically different conceptions of future city development.[36] The first was predicated on the continuation of Soviet-era levels of population growth over a twenty-year period, projecting a population increase to more than 700,000 residents. Of all new housing construction, 10 percent would be in the form of free-standing individual homes. The second projection foresaw the maintenance of the current status quo, with little or no population increase. The planners urged local officials to take advantage of stability to shift the profile of new housing construction away from large apartment houses. Hence, the second conception called for new housing construction to be distributed between 20 percent houses and 80 percent apartment buildings. The third proposed conception for the Yaroslavl of 2014 foresaw a radical deindustrialization and deurbanization of the entire region. The city's population would decline to around 580,000 inhabitants, while 40 percent of all new housing would take the form of single-family houses with garden plots. Financial incentives would be used to encourage city residents to return to the countryside and "reruralize" the city and province.

The problems of rural Yaroslavl are acute. Of the region's 1913 population, 85 percent lived in rural areas; this figure had dropped to 18 percent in 1991. Population density in rural areas fell from 28 persons per square kilometer to just 7 during the same period. While the agricultural population of the region actually increased slightly between 1989 and 1991, the number of pensioners remained 1.4 times higher than the number of children. Meanwhile, the death rate surpassed the birth rate, so that the recent modest population increase in the region's countryside is derived solely through migration. Those who remained on the farm have had a more difficult time in earning a living as low-value

[35] As reported in interview, Bobovich, September 1, 1992.
[36] Ibid., April 15, 1993.

fodder crops, which increased from 5 percent of regional agricultural output in 1913 to 57 percent in 1991, have come to replace more valuable agricultural products. Grain production, for example, decreased from 71 percent to 36 percent of total regional agricultural output between 1913 and 1991, while flax fell from 14 percent to 3 percent.[37]

All of these various concerns were raised when the mini-council debated the new general plan in September 1993.[38] The Moscow authors of the alternative development strategies presented their three projections for Yaroslavl's future. A hearty discussion followed, with a great deal of sympathy being expressed for a reduction in the city's size. However, deputies dismissed the idea of a smaller city as unrealistic. Instead, they instructed the Office of the Chief Architect to work with the Moscow consultants to develop more detailed projections of physical and economic trends under both the "no growth" and the "moderate growth" strategies. Additional documentation was to be prepared for further discussion on October 15, 1993. The suspension of the Russian Parliament in late September, followed by the insurrection of October 3–4, 1993, further delayed consideration of local general plans in Yaroslavl. With the mini-council disbanded and public attention directed toward the December 12, 1993, parliamentary elections and constitutional referendum, Mayor Volonchunas shied away from resolving the debate on his own.[39] Favoring some forum for public discussion, he concluded that the choice of future city planning strategies would have to await the establishment of new municipal institutions in 1994.[40]

CITY PLANNERS VERSUS REGIONAL PLANNERS

Despite the unresolved nature of the efforts to formulate a new general plan, the exercise reveals some significant departures from Soviet-era planning practices. Unlike in the past, the process has been largely transparent—with little effort being made to classify documents or otherwise conceal them from public view. City planners did not consult with economic officials before setting out to consider their city's future. Yet, some continuities remain. At the same moment that urban planners were

---

[37]These data are from Tat'iana Nefedova, "Iaroslavskoe selo," *Vash vybor*, 1993, no. 1 (January), pp. 10–11.
[38]Interview, Bobovich, September 9, 1993.
[39]Interview, Rumiantseva, November 10, 1993.
[40]Information obtained from Yaroslavl officials by Jeffrey Hahn of Villanova University through telephone communications on October 25, 1993.

Figure 30. Yaroslavl Regional Administration Building. Photograph by Blair A. Ruble.

beginning to evaluate the implications of radical deindustrialization, Regional Chief Administrator Anatolii Lisitsyn—sitting in the regional executive building across Soviet Square from the local "White House" (Figure 30)—initiated his own planning initiative for the entire oblast. He did so without consulting municipal officials, even though his ideas would have enormous consequence for the city. Such disregard for city authority by higher-ranking officials and institutions is unfortunately reminiscent of the not-very-distant Soviet past.

Lisitsyn was appointed by President Yeltsin as the chief of the Yaroslavl Regional Administration (or as "governor," in popular parlance) in December 1991, after having previously served as the mayor of nearby Rybinsk and as director of a local furniture factory.[41] Although he has vigorously fended off challenges from defenders of the old Communist Party, Lisitsyn is not widely regarded as a strong advocate of reform. Indeed, many local political observers view him as the captive of both

[41]Anatolii Lisitsyn, "Ne nado boiat'sia delit' polnomochiia," *Vash vybor,* 1992, no. 11 (November), pp. 6–7.

the region's powerful agricultural lobby (the *agrarniki*) and the directors of local military-industrial enterprises.[42]

Lisitsyn has sought to identify sources of economic growth within the region. This approach stood in contrast to the recommendations of lower-ranking regional officials who spoke at that time in rather dramatic terms of draining the massive Rybinsk reservoir, closing down that reservoir's hydroelectric dam, and returning to the flax and dairy farm regional economy of the pre-Soviet period.[43]

In late 1992, well after the city's planning project had been launched, Lisitsyn's "team" established a new information-analytical administration to gather data about the region.[44] By the spring of 1993, Lisitsyn invited the consulting firm of Yegor Gaidar, the then out-of-favor former Russian prime minister, to undertake development planning for the oblast as a whole.[45]

Lisitsyn and Gaidar identified Yaroslavl's central location along traditional trade and transportation routes as perhaps the region's single greatest comparative advantage. Rail lines, roads, pipe lines, and waterways converge on the city, as they have for centuries. Local officials added to this well-developed transportation infrastructure when they successfully gained permission to convert a local air force base to civilian use.[46] Consequently, the Gaidar-led team of consultants proposed the construction of a major international airport just outside of the city of Yaroslavl to serve Moscow and the Central Volga Region.[47]

Using bureaucratic and political connections, Lisitsyn and Gaidar successfully gained the endorsement of the appropriate Russian Federation ministries in Moscow to develop "Sheremetovo-3" (in a reference to the Moscow airports of that name) on Yaroslavl land. Yet, several major obstacles remain before work can begin on this mammoth project. First, little attention has been paid to the question of how the region might secure the huge capital investment required to bring the existing military

---

[42]Interview, Mizulin, September 9, 1993, and confirmed in numerous informal discussions with local officials.

[43]Interview, Ponomarev and Bushuev, April 14, 1993.

[44]Interview, Lisitsyn, April 15, 1993; interview, Guseev, April 13, 15, 1993; interview, Bushuev and Ponomarev, April 14, 1993; Anatolii Lisitsyn et al., "Regional'naia politika: opyt i printsipy," *Vash vybor*, 1993, no. 1 (January), pp. 34–35.

[45]Interview, Lisitsyn and Guseev, April 15, 1993; Aleksandr Bekker, "Iaroslavl' ishchet mesto v zhizni," *Segodnia*, July 6, 1993, p. 3.

[46]Interview, Gennadi Bykov, First Deputy Chief of Yaroslavl Regional Administration, Yaroslavl, September 8, 1993.

[47]This account is based on a number of off-the-record conversations as well as on interview, Bobovich, September 9, 1993.

airfield up to international civilian aviation standards. The money-starved Russian Federation government was similarly hard-pressed to secure the deficient capital. Second, Moscow-bound passengers will demand smooth and efficient transportation to the capital—a task far beyond current rail and highway capacities. Third, the proposed airport is only some ten miles from the Zavolzhskii residential districts constructed during the 1980s. Planners at that time could afford the luxury of being unconcerned with citizen activism. This is no longer the case. Local neighborhood leaders have already begun to mobilize against the Lisitsyn-Gaidar plan. Finally, regional officials apparently failed to inform city officials of the projected airport, thereby guaranteeing entrenched bureaucratic opposition from below.

The oblast planning initiative continues the Soviet-era tradition of establishing large-scale aggregate economic goals while leaving the details of consequent physical and social patterns for architects and city planners to worry about later on. The Lisitsyn-Gaidar consultants demonstrated an equally Soviet-style disregard for local officials and public opinion. For their part, Yaroslavl municipal planners started their quest for a development strategy by asking what kind of city they wanted to inhabit. They turned to the economic consequences of their decisions only later. This pattern reversed the Soviet-era pattern, according to which all physical planning decisions were held in abeyance until after the adoption of economy-dominated "technical-economic foundations" (TEO). These differences reflect the lingering Soviet bureaucratic ethos of many regional politicians and administrators, as well as the somewhat greater flexibility of their city-level counterparts.

In Moscow, similarly sharp differences between the autonomous Moscow city and Moscow regional administrations led President Yeltsin to organize a new "associational council" *(ob"edinenie kollegiia),* bringing together representatives of the city and the region to coordinate policies of mutual interest.[48] The purpose of this new body is to encourage officials from throughout the Moscow metropolitan area to consult with one another. The council's decisions were merely consultative to both city and regional administrators and legislators. It nonetheless eased some of the confusion over joint policy concerns—such as land use in the Moscow greenbelt—which previously would have been sub-

[48]Interview, Kemer Borisovich Norkin, General Director, Department of the Mayor, Moscow, and Chair, Associational Council of Moscow City and Moscow Region, Moscow, September 13, 1993.

ject to the overarching management and supervision of Communist Party agencies.

All post-Soviet planning projections in Yaroslavl have had an air of unreality about them. Regional capital resources for local investment are in acutely short supply. Some local officials are betting heavily on German capital to spur development.[49] The prominent Yarkassel joint venture has already been mentioned, as have the thriving sister-city and sister-region relationships with Germany. The German state of Hessen recently opened a permanent representational office in Yaroslavl.[50] Yet, there is no local financial infrastructure to channel or administer investment. Those Moscow banks that have attempted to initiate financial services in Yaroslavl—especially for home mortgages and small business loans—have reputedly been driven away by strongly protectionist networks of regional political and business leaders who fear outside competition and interference in their affairs.

Serious problems would remain for the implementation of any plan even if the financial infrastructure could be put into place to support local development. As Yaroslavl City Chief Architect Arkady Bobovich noted during an interview, any attempt to reorganize living patterns around individual houses—or commerce around small businesses—faces immediate economic and technological obstacles.[51] In the housing sector alone, a local construction industry oriented toward single-family houses has yet to develop; and such an industry would require extensive legal and technical supports at the cost of millions of scarce rubles before it could survive.

Perhaps most important, projections of rustic semirural city dwellers tending to their gardens by night and of their country cousins milking cows and cutting flax by day ignore the terrible environmental degradation of the Soviet era. Heavy metal soil pollution would have to be attacked at considerable expense before Yaroslavtsy could even contemplate tending their own gardens. Finally, population projections are

---

[49]Interview, Guseev, April 13, 1993; interview, Zharikov, Director, Department of Foreign Economic Activities, Yaroslavl Regional Administration, Yaroslavl, September 7, 1993.
[50]Interview, Zharikov, September 7, 1993.
[51]Interview, Bobovich, April 15, 1993.

erroneous at times of great social upheaval.[52] Whether the city's population expands or contracts will depend on the future success of Russian
economic and political reform, as well as on the country's capacity to
absorb tens of thousands of demobilized soldiers and refugees fleeing
ethnic conflicts to the south and east.

Regardless of such obvious difficulties, the variety and inventiveness
of the various physical and economic conceptions under discussion
throughout the early 1990s for the city and region of Yaroslavl demonstrated an intense desire to use the opportunity posed by the collapse
of central authority in Moscow to chart a unique local destiny, one that
would serve Yaroslavtsy and not Muscovites. Whatever the practical
difficulties of implementation, each of these projections revealed the extent to which local officials have sought to reinvent their city. City authorities did not remain idle while they sorted out competing visions for
Yaroslavl's distant future. They moved forward simultaneously with
their Moscow colleagues to initiate a zoning code and to identify areas
for the construction of single-family housing.

According to Bobovich, the absence of zoning regulations posed an
immediate concern to city officials.[53] Soviet-era land-use regulations
were poorly written, and enforcement mechanisms were nonexistent.
Consequently, city officials did not quite know how to proceed with
regulating privately owned property. New owners, for their part, firmly
believed that title would transfer total authority over a particular building or site. Bitter fights erupted following the conversion to commercial
use of some of the initial twenty or so single-family dwellings built in
the city. Neighbors were outraged when the owner of one particularly
expensive house turned it into an auto repair station. The local procurator's office has been unable to enforce land-use regulations, and city
officials fear that such conflicts over land use will only increase in the
future. The mayor's office has been considering the implementation of
various dispute-mediation mechanisms for some time, but conflicts continue to arise.

FINDING A PLACE FOR A HOME

Rather than wait for a new general plan or a zoning code, planning
authorities in some Russian cities, including Yaroslavl, established spe-

---

[52]Interview, Rumiantseva, April 15, 1993; interview, Bobovich, April 15, 1993.
[53]Interview, Bobovich, September 1, 1992, and April 15, 1993.

cial areas for the construction of single-family dwellings in an effort to direct the city's development. In mid-1992, for example, the Leningrad Region established a special zone, extending fifty to seventy kilometers around the St. Petersburg city limits, in which 250,000 building sites were set aside for the construction of single-family houses.[54] In Yaroslavl, local officials invited specialists from Moscow's Central Scientific Research and Design Institute for City Construction to work with them throughout the summer of 1992 to similarly identify tracts of land suitable for residential developments.[55] Two areas in the Zavolzhskii District were deemed acceptable for immediate development; a third, just beyond the city's western planning boundary, was set aside for future growth. All three sites were far removed from lower-income areas, in the hope that the social conflict that surged during the construction of the city's first single-family houses might be alleviated.

Both the Zavolzhskii sites—one to the north and the other to the south of the existing high-rise neighborhoods built during the 1970s and 1980s—are under the control of state farms *(sovkhozy)* eager to capitalize on real estate development. Nearby stands of trees ensure a congenial setting, and all the tracts are considered to be relatively pollution-free.

Designs for the new "cottages" resemble modest American suburban homes of the late 1940s and early 1950s.[56] Many are to be built by factories for sale to their workers. City regulations require that 20 percent of all newly constructed single-family houses be reserved for sale to employees in health services and education because institutions in those sectors lack the resources to construct housing on their own. Officials anticipate that middle-level managers will constitute the largest single purchasing group, since senior managers already have decent housing and since lower professional ranks cannot afford to purchase or main-

---

[54]Dychinskii, "Chelovek i sreda obitaniia," p. 27.

[55]Interview, Bobovich, September 1, 1992, and April 15, 1993.

[56]This similarity may not be accidental. Moscow Architectural Institute Professor Dmitrii Shvidkovskii reported that his students copy plans for private houses out of American magazines (interview, Dmitrii Shvidkovskii, Professor, Moscow Architectural Institute, Moscow, April 20, 1993) in a pattern that has long been repeated in Russia during the late Imperial era (see William C. Brumfield, "Russian Perceptions of American Architecture, 1870–1918," in William C. Brumfield, ed., *Reshaping Russian Architecture: Western Technology, Utopian Dreams* [Cambridge: Cambridge University Press, 1990], pp. 43–66) and in the Stalin era (Stephen Kotkin, "Shelter and Subjectivity in the Stalin Period: A Case Study of Magnitogorsk," in Brumfield and Ruble, *Russian Housing in the Modern Age*, pp. 171–210).

Figure 31. New housing construction, Yaroslavl, 1991. Photograph by Blair A. Ruble.

tain their own dwellings.[57] Sale prices were set to begin at R2.5 million ($12,195 in September 1992) for a typical two-story structure with an additional basement and a mansard roof attic (Figure 31). This price represented a tenfold increase over the original selling prices of the city's first single-family structures offered for sale a year before, in September 1991 (R250,000 or $2,000 at that time). Even so, the price was probably well below market value given that private developers were selling fully furnished, two- and three-story brick homes in the northern suburb of Norsk for between $75,000 and $100,000 (payable in cash in dollars) in early 1993.[58]

Despite all of the post-Soviet economic uncertainties—including the very likely prospect of bankruptcy—Yaroslavl factories continued to plan and to initiate construction of worker "cottage settlements," based on American suburban plan books of two and three decades ago. Municipal authorities encouraged such development both to direct similar economic groups into closer proximity with one another and to encour-

[57]Interview, Bobovich, September 1, 1992, and April 15, 1993.
[58]Tour of Yaroslavl City housing sites, April 14, 1993.

age large-scale investment in local housing. Yet, once again, democratic customs and norms have yet to be fully absorbed by local public and private industrialists. Long accustomed to having their way, managers at Avtodizel' decided that the best site for their new worker cottages was a very popular wooded park overlooking the Volga. Their land-grab would have succeeded had it not been for city council deputies who recoiled in fear following the angry protests of their newly mobilized constituents. For the first time in Yaroslavtsy's memory, Avtodizel' failed to get a request approved by local authorities.[59]

Yaroslavl officials remain concerned over the provision of transportation and infrastructural support for these new communities.[60] They question the local conventional wisdom that it will not be necessary to provide public transportation to housing tracts because "people who can afford a house can afford a car." They worry about the adequacy of the city's road system and argue convincingly that a second trans-Volga bridge south of the Kotorosl'-Volga confluence must be completed by the year 2010. Budgeting and planning for this new span have begun, but continuing economic and political uncertainties threaten construction. Of equal importance, they argue in favor of municipal involvement in the construction of new highways, sewers, and water systems as a means of exercising control over future development patterns.[61] If the city permits construction firms and factories to decide where and how infrastructural facilities will be constructed, they contend, the city will be able to exercise little or no control over future development.

A POLITICS OF PROPERTY LIKE MANY OTHERS

By the summer of 1993, the question of municipal oversight, control, and taxation gained importance in a new controversy that is all too familiar to city leaders in the United States. The effort to prepare a new general plan had led, quite unexpectedly, to the discovery that the municipality had never bothered to establish formal boundaries between

[59]Interview, Rumiantseva, April 15, 1993; interview, Bobovich, April 15, 1993.
[60]Interview, Bobovich, September 1, 1992, and April 15, 1993.
[61]Concern over the control of highways, for example, prompted the classification and distribution of maintenance responsibility for roads throughout the region in early 1992 (Malyi sovet Iaroslavskogo gorodskogo soveta narodnykh deputatov, "Reshenie No. 231 o klassifikatsii avtomobil'nykh dorog v Iaroslavskoi oblasti, ot 26 fevralia 1992 g." [February 26, 1992]).

itself and the surrounding countryside.[62] Apparently, no one had attempted to address the issue because, under the old administrative system, formal boundaries between jurisdictions never mattered very much.[63] The mayor's office proposed that the mini-council merely ratify the planning boundaries of the Brezhnev-era Yaroslavl general plan as the municipality's official boundaries. This move would have incorporated a number of small, fringe agricultural settlements into city boundaries. Relatively prosperous by local standards, the residents of these communities wanted nothing to do with city regulations and city taxes. Anticipating growing revenues from the sale and lease of farmlands to new home owners, nearby state farms *(sovkhozy)* similarly unleashed every possible defense against what they perceived as the city's great landgrab of 1993. Charges of payoffs and bribes lingered in the air as the mini-council, over the course of the summer, failed to approve any city boundaries. As with many other unresolved planning issues, the city's capacity to establish its administrative boundaries and capture tax revenues from the surrounding countryside must now await the emergence of stable political and administrative structures in its post-Soviet future.

As the transition from central planning toward markets and democratic institutions continues, planners in Yaroslavl—as in other market economies—have become increasingly anxious about the power of private capital in shaping their city's physical development. The preparation of a new general plan must be substantially different from any such effort in the past. The resulting planning objectives and implementation mechanisms will shape municipal administrators' relationship to the private sector. Land-use planning promises to be one arena in which the issues of urban space will determine the shape of post-Soviet politics in Yaroslavl.

[62]Interview, Vladimir Bakaev, Deputy Chair, Yaroslavl City Soviet, Yaroslavl, September 7, 1993; interview, Bobovich, September 9, 1993.
[63]This state of affairs helps to explain the numerous boundary disputes among the post-Soviet successor states.

Conclusion:
The post-Soviet city and Russian democracy

On October 23, 1993, the attention of the world press—or, at least, of that small part of the world press based in Moscow—focused on Yaroslavl. Boris Yeltsin, making his first major political appearance since the tragic events at the Russian Parliament three weeks before, joined political and religious leaders from the Russian Federation, Belarus, and Ukraine in the shabby square at the front of Yaroslavl's main post office. There, in the frost of an early-autumn afternoon, they dedicated a new monument to Yaroslav the Wise, prince of the Kievan Rus', creator of the first written Slavic legal code, and founder of the city of Yaroslavl (Figure 32).[1]

The statue itself had provoked something of a controversy in the city.[2] Its cost of $40,000 struck some as an extravagance, given the city's severe fiscal constraints. Others argued bitterly about the statue's design. The largest group of critics merely urged that Yaroslav be moved to the site, overlooking the Volga, where legend has it that he defeated a bear in a famous wrestling match in 1010.[3]

City officials already had grown accustomed to such disputes. Discussions over a new design for the city's seal had dragged on for months. The city council had been paralyzed by discussions of the historic authenticity of the seal, of the precise position of this paw or that

---

[1]Craig R. Whitney, "Yeltsin Appears in Public to Honor a Hero of the Past," *New York Times,* October 24, 1993, p. 12; "Segodnia—otkrytie pamiatnika Iaroslavu Mudromu," *Severnyi krai,* October 23, 1993, p. 1; "V oblastnoi administratsii," p. 1.

[2]Interview, Bakaev, September 9, 1993; interview, Belaev, September 9, 1993; interview, Bobovich, September 9, 1993; interview, Rumiantseva, September 9, 1993.

[3]An account of the city's founding myth—and of the famous wrestling match between Yaroslav and a bear—may be found in V. Khrapchenko, "Stranitsy istorii: Vstrecha so 'skazaniem o postroenii grada Iaroslavlia,' " *Severnyi krai,* October 23, 1993, p. 1.

127

Figure 32. Monument to Yaroslav the Wise. Photograph by Peggy McInerny.

of the dominant bear on the herald, of the size and shape of the ax tossed over the bear's shoulder, and of the appropriate balance between warning and welcome in the bear's grin.[4] This time, city officials formed a blue ribbon commission, inviting leading cultural, civic, and religious

[4]Interview, Bakaev, April 13, 1993, and September 9, 1993.

figures from Yaroslavl, Belarus, and Ukraine to participate in their deliberations.[5] Convinced that they had finally figured out how to run such competitions, they were lulled into a false sense of security by the scanty press coverage and mild public interest in their discussions.

The city's architects and planners had decided to draw on European design principles to bring some modicum of order to the sprawling, ill-defined open space in front of the city post office. The "square," left over from an awkward juncture of the Catherinian and subsequent street patterns, had presented something of a design problem. A relatively recent bridge across the Kotorosl' dumped arriving traffic from Moscow into a rather large, typical Russian trading *dvor*. This disorder *(bezobrazie)* simply would not do in a city striving for increased tourism from abroad. Hence, the city decided to place the monument in a traffic circle that would provide a focal point to the rather awkward public space greeting tourists arriving in their cars. The only problem was that many Yaroslavtsy—unschooled in the architectural principles of the Italian Renaissance—rather enjoyed their ungainly square. Distinct Russian and Western notions of urban space had once again come into conflict.

The placement of public statuary has long been controversial in Russia.[6] The concept of stand-alone monuments, an idea imported by the Westernizing regimes of the eighteenth century, remains alien to Russian tradition. Aside from the rather prominent Lenin statues of the Soviet period, most Russian public monuments are pushed off into some corner or other of the city. That is precisely what the local citizenry proposed to do with Yaroslav the Wise—put him out on the bluff overlooking the confluence of the Volga and Kotorosl' rivers for the tourists to see.

City authorities had their way in the end, and Yaroslav the Lawgiver now provides a modicum of Western-style rationality to a main public space in central Yaroslavl. The aesthetic principles of the professionals won out over populist impulses. City leaders hungry for tourist rubles, dollars, marks, and pounds made their choice. A beleaguered President Yeltsin, looking for an opportunity to underline the fact that the Eastern Slavs share a common past, bestowed his approval on their decision before the television cameras of local, national, and international news companies. New form was given to a prominent neighborhood in this

---

[5]These figures included, it should be noted, representatives of the Orthodox Church in Russia and Ukraine as well as of the Ukrainian Uniate Church.
[6]Interview, Glazychev, September 11, 1993.

ancient Russian town. Fittingly, in a reference to iconographic tradition, Yaroslav cradles a model of the city in his arms.[7]

A MOMENT OF URBAN REINVENTION

An examination of urban form and the processes by which it has come into being reveals a great deal about its creators. The building of a city involves every aspect of human existence. It blends the economic with the political, as well as the social with the cultural, into the material expression of otherwise abstract and remote "tendencies" and "forces."

The shaping of a city places societal changes in particularly sharp relief. The physical order of the city undergoes continuous modification, even in as small a detail as the shape of a lamppost. Indeed, one sign of hope for many Yaroslavtsy during the present-day "time of troubles" is that "historically accurate" lampposts have been installed throughout the center of town.

Of perhaps greater importance, people's understanding of the city in general—and of a specific city in particular—evolves even as the physical environment remains more or less constant. Kevin Lynch observed in 1959 that the city is not only "an object which is perceived (and perhaps enjoyed) by millions of people of widely diverse class and character, but it is the product of many builders who are constantly modifying the structure for reasons of their own."[8] The result for Jonathan Raban is an "emporium of style" in which "there is no single point of view from which one can grasp the city as a whole."[9] The public nature of the urban environment permits the observer to penetrate the various influences shaping that world.

Lynch and Raban both assumed that cities are the public manifestation of an infinite number of private visions and decisions. The city is imagined by thousands—resident and visitor, official and citizen. An examination of the principles and motivations underlying their decisions exposes the public and private forces that shape society. Russia's Soviet experience, however, devalued the standing of private decisions in shaping the urban form. State agencies and government planners appropri-

---

[7]This gesture immediately prompted local wags to nickname the statue *Iaroslav s tortom* (Yaroslav with a Cake).
[8]Kevin Lynch, *The Image of the City* (Cambridge, Mass.: MIT Press, 1959), p. 2.
[9]Jonathan Raban, *Soft City* (London: Harvill/HarperCollins, 1988), p. 242.

ated city building as their own. The dreariness, tedium, and banality of the modern Russian city is a natural consequence of this appropriation.

The devolution of political and economic decision-making that has marked the past half-decade or so elevates the importance of individual choice in shaping the future Russian city. Any movement, no matter how irregular, toward the creation of market mechanisms in the Russian economy will carry with it both a new set of problems all too familiar to Western city dwellers and, of perhaps greater significance in the current Russian context, a renewed opportunity for the private realm to gain pride of place in urban development. One lesson from this study, then, is that profits and property will grow in importance as Russian cities respond to a more market-oriented system of economic organization. Money will matter more and more in this moment of urban reinvention.

THE TRANSITIONAL CITY

The politics of property stand at the center of the conflict over the role of the state in Russia's future. Only the state can shape the city in a world without individual or corporate property rights. At present, the who, what, when, where, and how of property relations in a new Russia have yet to be established. The resolution of these questions is becoming visible even in the very stones of but a single provincial Russian city. Examining these processes in Yaroslavl may disclose valuable insights into the social, cultural, political, and economic forces shaping Russia more generally. Three clusters of issues have already emerged that revolve around debates over the future shape of the city.

Housing will be privatized as the municipality and the various enterprises that currently control and manage apartment buildings seek to divest their responsibilities to residents. Quarrels are erupting across Russia over the most just distribution of responsibility and cost among state agencies and individual citizens and their families. Participants in these discussions appear only dimly concerned about the psychological, economic, and political consequences of private custody over the primal resource of shelter. Even those who are familiar with American debates over property taxes, mortgage deductions on income tax, and the myriad other issues that rouse home owners can only begin to imagine the transformation of Russian political and economic life that will follow in the wake of the privatization of state housing.

The tension between the aesthetic and commercial prerogatives of historic preservation are visible now more than ever. Debates swirl around specific projects while preservation authorities attempt to define appropriate functions in an environment that requires profit. Preservation activists and architects throughout the world would recognize these dilemmas and conflicts. Yaroslavtsy must devise their own means for managing and resolving conflicts that were previously preempted by state planners in Moscow.

Land-use and urban planning decisions that have ignored financial constraints are giving way to a new preoccupation with land cost. Planners must learn how to incorporate private actors into their vision of Yaroslavl's future. Enterprise managers must recalculate how much land they should occupy to accomplish their economic mission. Where people live and work will be quite different in the years to come as hundreds and thousands of individual and institutional decisions find expression in the city's physical form.

Each of these policy areas demonstrates the extent to which the post-Soviet city is transitional. Privatization of housing moved forward in fits and starts before grinding to a halt altogether under the weight of the contradictory high politics leading to the collapse of Russia's first post-Soviet republic in late 1993. Title to approximately one-fifth of state apartments was turned over to residents during the two years following the collapse of Soviet power. Even when residents gained title, individual apartments remained physically embedded in huge buildings and neighborhoods based on a socialized infrastructure. Single-family houses are being built, yet they remain tied to an urban order long hostile to individual dwellings. Prices are established by municipal planners as much as by market mechanisms. The transition to a private-dominated housing market will be long. Nevertheless, the physical form of Yaroslavl is already being transformed by the privatization of municipal and enterprise apartments and the construction of single-family cottage settlements. A new, decentralized, boundless urban form, well known to urban and suburban residents of capitalist societies, is coming into being. The precise contours of this future post-Soviet city may not yet be well defined, but the vague outline can already be discerned.

The importance and function of historic preservation in the post-Soviet city are similarly muddled. A broad preservationist coalition that united in its opposition to local Communist potentates has fractured. Bitter disputes, all too familiar to Western preservation groups, have erupted between those who view preservation as an economic development strategy and those who seek cultural definition. Yet, post-Soviet Russia is different. An intense battle rages over the meaning of the Russian past. Discussions over the proper disposition of state-controlled religious monuments have become one of several flash points in this larger contest. Simultaneously, uncertainty over the prerogatives of private ownership has led to barbed court battles. More fully developed and refined notions of the relationship between the modern post-Soviet city and its pre-Soviet historic core eventually will take shape out of these continuing encounters. Financial considerations will matter more than ever in preservation.

The post-Soviet transition has created a valuable opportunity for Russian citizens, officials, and planners to reinvent their towns. An entire range of physical planning issues long shrouded in Soviet-era security regulations has become exposed to public discussion. Should Yaroslavl expand or contract? Should its housing pattern remain tied to public transportation? Should rich live next to poor? Where should industry be located? If factories are to close, by what should they be replaced? How will municipal authorities manage urban development if money determines behavior?

Yaroslavtsy have been presented with a rare chance to rethink their community, to reinvent its physical form, and to reimagine its future. They have pursued this opportunity with zeal, offering up an impressive assortment of economic and physical visions ranging from an unrealistic longing for a lost agricultural past—complete with dismantling a major hydroelectric dam—to equally unrealistic visions of a high-tech future. If only urbanites in less transitional systems had the same possibilities to dream! Yet, once again, the harsh truths of the first post-Soviet republic press down, grinding local deliberations to a halt while national leaders in Moscow sort out their preferred constitutional arrangements for the Russian Federation. One lesson from this study, then, is that center and periphery must work in concert for new policies to be successfully implemented.

THE IMPORTANCE OF REGIONAL PERSPECTIVES

Much of the rethinking of Yaroslavl has been a consequence of the collapse of the central Russian state. The heavy hand of central bureaucracy has been lifted, leaving municipal and regional officials to deal with daily reality more or less on their own. The paralysis of power in Moscow, together with the very transitional character of the post-Soviet period, has created a singular opportunity for local residents. Local customs and folkways now inform urban decision-making to an extent simply unthinkable a decade ago.

A regional culture of *po tikhon'ku*—of merely typical rather than exemplary performance—has united Yaroslavtsy in a desire to make their community work. When asked why the politics of compromise has dominated the local political scene, People's Deputy Father Mikhail Peregudov responded that "ambitious people leave for Moscow" and that those who remain behind "lack political pretension." Most of all, "Yaroslavtsy want their children to live better than they have."[10] Two and one-half years later, Anatolii Lisitsyn, chief (or governor) of the Yaroslavl Regional Administration, expressed a similar thought in different words when he explained that the purpose of local government is to "cushion the impact of reform."[11]

Such attitudes have fostered a cautious attitude toward reform. Kathryn Stoner-Weiss, in a dissertation comparing reform strategies in several Russian regions, concludes that, according to a variety of performance indicators, Yaroslavl consistently ranks in the middle of those regions examined.[12] Yet, this same circumspection sustains a local "politics of good will" that has frequently shielded Yaroslavl from many of the upheavals in Moscow over the course of the first republic. The local government opposed the August 1991 putsch almost immediately, and during a period of rising tensions before the April 1993 referendum, representatives of all local political groups and institutions gathered quietly to explore ways to avoid violence in the region.[13] Everyone—private citizen, military officer, bureaucrat, and elected official alike, it seems—kept out of sight during the October 1993 confrontation between President Yeltsin and the insurrectionist Parliament led by Aleksandr Rutskoi and Ruslan Khasbulatov. Regional leaders Anatolii Lisitsyn and Aleksandr Veselov immediately appealed for calm after shooting broke out in Moscow, declaring their intent not to repeat the bloody confrontation between executive and legislature on the local level.[14] Rather than sub-

---

[10]Interview, Peregudov, December 13, 1990.
[11]Interview, Lisitsyn and Guseev, April 15, 1993.
[12]Stoner-Weiss, "Local Heroes."
[13]Interview, Bakaev, April 13, 1993.
[14]Anatolii Lisitsyn, "Obrashchenie A. I. Lisitsyna," *Severnyi krai*, October 5, 1993, p. 1; A. N. Veselov, "Obrashchenie A. N. Veselova," *Severnyi krai*, October 5, 1993, p. 1.

vert political reform, this underlying tolerance and desire for compromise has sustained a regional political culture supportive of democratic institutions.[15]

Robert Putnam has written eloquently on the critical role played by regional political traditions and cultures in sustaining democratic institutions. In *Making Democracy Work: Civic Tradition in Modern Italy,* Putnam wrote: "Social context and history profoundly condition the effectiveness of institutions. Where the regional soil is fertile, the regions draw sustenance from regional traditions, but where the soil is poor, the new institutions are stunted. . . . For political stability, for government effectiveness, and even for economic progress social capital may be even more important than physical or human capital."[16] Provincial Russia has traditionally been thought of as a place where the soil is especially barren for democratic politics. The sort of dense network of horizontal social organizations described by Putnam as the social capital for democratic life has not been particularly evident in Russian life. Yet, as the case of Yaroslavl demonstrates, there exists an underlying political culture of tolerance, on which such social capital may be nurtured.

Russia is reinventing itself, with regions and localities such as Yaroslavl struggling to answer defining questions: Who will control Russia's enormous natural wealth? Who will determine and control local revenues? What revenues will be allocated to the center? Who will determine local economic and physical development? And, most especially, *what* is Russia and *who* are the Russians? The traditional center-periphery relationship between Moscow and the Russian provinces is being transformed by this struggle; already dissimilar from its Soviet version, the post-Soviet relationship may be wholly redefined within a decade by communities such as Yaroslavl. One lesson of this study, then, is that only local officials can turn policy pronouncement into local reality, since it is they who must try to square the circle between abstract economic models and everyday life.

Despite all of the obvious caveats about the dangers of generalizing from a single case, many lessons may be gleaned from an effort to examine the politics of urban space in a provincial Russian city during the

[15]Jeffrey W. Hahn, "The Evolution of Local Legislatures: The Case of Yaroslavl' " (paper presented at the conference "Democratization in Russia: The Development of Legislative Institutions," Harvard University, Cambridge, Mass., October 29–30, 1993).

[16]Robert Putnam, *Making Democracy Work: Civic Tradition in Modern Italy* (Princeton: Princeton University Press, 1993), pp. 182–83.

first post-Soviet republic in Russia. Yaroslavtsy of all social ranks struggled to reinvent their city and, in the process, demonstrated an appreciation that their future cannot be like their past. They may have wanted to proceed to a new post-Soviet city slowly, they may have wanted to be respectful of Soviet-era social programs, and they may have resisted privatization of their apartments. Nevertheless, they did change.

The growth of civil society and democratic political institutions was visibly apparent in post-Soviet Yaroslavl. It was precisely at the level of a single provincial town that the potential for a new democratic Russia became most unmistakable. In reimagining the physical form of their city, Yaroslavtsy were also reimagining the political form of their community.

His tie was now loosened, his eyes and face redder and puffier than two hours before. With the vodka and cognac depleted, the veneer of feigned European respectability long since gone, he slammed down his tumbler after the traditional last drink for the road, leaned forward, and whispered loudly, "Invest your money here in Russia, not in America. *U nas*, here, with us, *den'gi ne govoriat*, money does not talk, *den'gi poiut*, money sings!"

Selected bibliography

INTERVIEWS

Abaiushkin, Leonid Iur'evich. Deputy, Moscow City Soviet; Member, Moscow City Soviet Commission on the Media. Washington, D.C., February 4, 1991.

Agafonov, Nikolai Timofeevich. Senior Researcher, Institute of Socio-Economic Problems, USSR Academy of Sciences. Leningrad, February 20, 1984.

Andropov, Sergei Nikolaevich. People's Deputy, Russian Federation Supreme Soviet. Washington, D.C., August 4, 1992.

Anisimov, Evgenii Viktorovich. Senior Researcher, Institute of History, Russian Academy of Sciences. St. Petersburg, September 11, 1991.

Ankudinova, Elena Andreevna. Director, Architectural Division, Yaroslavl City Museum. Yaroslavl, June 25, 1990.

Baikova, Lidia Ivanovna. Environmental Activist. Yaroslavl, June 19, 1990 (with leaders of Yaroslavl People's Front); Yaroslavl, June 22, 1990.

Bakaev, Vladimir Nikolaevich. First Deputy Chair, Yaroslavl City Soviet. Yaroslavl, June 20, 1990 (with Kruglikov); Yaroslavl, December 11, 1990 (with Kruglikov); Yaroslavl, October 11, 1991; Yaroslavl, April 28, 1992; Yaroslavl, September 4, 1992; Yaroslavl, April 13, 1993; Yaroslavl, September 7–9, 1993.

Barabash, Viktor Maksimovich. Retired First Secretary, Yaroslavl City Communist Party Committee; Secretary, Construction Affairs of the Yaroslavl Regional Communist Party Committee. Yaroslavl, June 26, 1990.

Baskov, Viktor Petrovich. Professor, Yaroslavl Pedagogical Institute; former Yaroslavl Regional Party Secretary. Yaroslavl, June 19, 1990; Yaroslavl, December 14, 1990.

Belaev, Iurii Vital'evich. Chief Engineer, Yaroslavl Regional Administration for the Preservation of Historic Monuments. Yaroslavl, September 9, 1993.

Boborykin, Pavel Grigor'evich. Deputy Director, Department of Culture, Yaroslavl Regional Executive Committee. Yaroslavl, June 25, 1990 (with Vasil'eva and Peregudov).

Bobovich, Arkady Romanovich. Chief Architect, Yaroslavl. Yaroslavl, October 11, 14, 1991; Yaroslavl, September 1, 1992; Yaroslavl, April 15, 1993; Yaroslavl, September 9, 1993.

Bocharov, Iurii Petrovich. Chairman, Soviet Society of Urbanists; Deputy Director for Research, Central Scientific Research and Design Institute for Town Planning (Moscow). Washington, D.C., March 22, 1991; Washington, D.C., May 9, 1991.

Bogordetskii, Vladimir Valentinovich. Chief Architect, Yaroslavl Region. Yaroslavl, June 22, 1990 (with Izanov and Bykov).

Bol'shakov, Aleksandr Alekseevich. Former First Deputy Chairman, Leningrad City Soviet; Chairman, Leningrad City Planning Commission. Leningrad, January 25, 1990.

Bushuev, Aleksei Vladimirovich. Deputy Chief, Regional Information-Analytical Administration, Yaroslavl Region. Yaroslavl, April 14, 1993 (with Ponomarev).

Bykov, Gennadi Stepanovich. First Deputy Chief, Yaroslavl Regional Administration. Yaroslavl, September 8, 1993 (with Zharikov).

Bykov, Vladimir Konstantinovich. Member, Architectural Planning Staff, Yaroslavl Region. Yaroslavl, June 22, 1990 (with Bogordetskii and Izanov).

Chervnikov, Iuzef Iakovlevich. Economic Director, Yaroslavl Motor Works Avtodizel'. Yaroslavl, April 29, 1992 (with Zheltyakov).

Chisnikov, Leonid Aleksandrovich. Editor-in-Chief, *Severnyi rabochii*. Yaroslavl, June 19, 1990.

Druzhinin, Dmitrii Leonidovich. Deputy, Gagarin District Soviet (Moscow); Member, Presidium of Soviet and Chairman of the Enterprise and Commercial Commission. Washington, D.C., April 23, 1991; Washington, D.C., May 16, 1991.

Ershov, Aleksandr Fedorovich. Yaroslavl Coordinator, Association of Regions and Cities of Central Districts of Russia. Yaroslavl, October 14, 1991.

Erzhova, Nadezhda Leonidovna. Head, Housing Privatization Office of Mayor of Yaroslavl. Yaroslavl, April 16, 1993; Yaroslavl, September 8, 1993.

Fadeev, Valerii Valerevich. Deputy, Moscow City Soviet. Washington, D.C., December 11–12, 1991; Washington, D.C., July 13, 1992.

Gaidis, Stanislav Konstantinovich. Member, Yaroslavl People's Front; Deputy to Yaroslavl Regional Soviet. Yaroslavl, June 19, 1990 (with other leaders of Yaroslavl People's Front); Yaroslavl, October 14, 1991.

Glazychev, Vyacheslav Leonidovich. President, Moscow Branch, European Academy of the Urban Environment. Moscow, August 25, 1992; Washington, D.C., May 5, 10, 1993; Moscow, September 4, 11, 1993.

Guseev, Anatolii Fedorovich. Deputy Chief Administrator, Yaroslavl Region. Yaroslavl, September 2–3, 1992; Washington, D.C., February 8–10, 1993; Yaroslavl, April 13, 15 (with Lisitsyn), 16, 1993; Washington, D.C., June 18, 1993.

Guseinov, Aidyn Akhmedovich. Member, Yaroslavl Environmental Research Group attached to Yaroslavl City Soviet. Yaroslavl, June 27, 1990; Yaroslavl, December 12, 1990.

Harchenko, Oleg Andreevich. Chief Architect, St. Petersburg Mayor's Office. Baltimore, Md., October 2, 1992; Baltimore, Md., June 23, 1993.

Istomina, Valentina Vladimirovna. Chief, Financial-Budget Department, Yaroslavl. Yaroslavl, October 11, 1991; Washington, D.C., November 7–9, 1993.

Ivanov, Valerii Sergeevich. Director, Yaroslavl International Business University. Yaroslavl, September 4, 1992.

Izanov, Vladimir Konstantinovich. Deputy Chief Architect, Yaroslavl Region. Yaroslavl, June 22, 1990 (with Bogordetskii and Bykov).

Kaganov, Grigorii Zosimovich. Department Head, All-Union Scientific Research Institute of the Theory of Architecture and City Planning. Moscow, June 9, 1990; Moscow, June 29, 1990; Moscow, December 8, 1990; Moscow, December 15, 1990; St. Petersburg, September 11–12, 1991; Moscow, October 8, 1991; Moscow, April 23, 1992; Moscow, May 1, 1992; Moscow, August

26, 1992; Moscow, April 11, 1993; Moscow, April 18, 1993; Moscow, September 5, 11, 1993.

Kaganova, Olga Zosimovna. Leading Scientific Worker, Leningrad Scientific Research Institute on the Theory of Architecture and City Planning; Specialist on Soviet Land Prices. Leningrad, January 23, 1990; Washington, D.C., October 22 (with Maslennikov), 23, 1991.

Kalinin, Sergei Aleksandrovich. First Secretary, Yaroslavl Regional Communist Party Committee. Yaroslavl, December 13, 1990.

Kolbatskii, Iulis Iakovlevich. First Deputy Chair, Yaroslavl Regional Soviet. Yaroslavl, June 19, 1990 (with Veselov); Yaroslavl, June 20, 1990.

Komarev, Ivan Ivanovich. Chief, Department of Privatization of Municipal Property, Fund of Municipal Property, Yaroslavl. Yaroslavl, September 8, 1993.

Kovalev, Vladimir Aleksandrovich. Deputy Mayor, Yaroslavl. Yaroslavl, September 4, 1992.

Kozliakov, Viacheslav Nikolaevich. Professor of History, Yaroslavl State University. Yaroslavl, December 13, 1990; Yaroslavl, October 15, 1991; Yaroslavl, April 28, 1992 (with Sevastianova); Yaroslavl, April 15, 1993.

Kruglikov, Lev Leonidovich. Chairman, Yaroslavl City Soviet. Yaroslavl, June 20, 1990 (with Bakaev); Yaroslavl, December 11, 1990 (with Bakaev); Yaroslavl, April 28, 1992; Washington, D.C., May 20, 1992; Yaroslavl, September 4, 1992; Washington, D.C., April 7, 1993.

Kugel', Samuel Aronovich. Professor, St. Petersburg University of Economics and Finance. Moscow, September 13, 1993.

Kuzmichev, Aleksandr Viktorovich. Architect, Office of the Moscow General Plan. Moscow, June 14, 1990.

Kuznetsov, Boris Nikolaevich. Deputy Chair, Yaroslavl City Executive Committee for Culture. Yaroslavl, June 22, 1990 (with Vinnichenko).

Lisitsyn, Anatolii Ivanovich. Chief of Regional Administration, Yaroslavl Region. Yaroslavl, April 15, 1993 (with Guseev).

Markovin, Iurii Borisovich. Leader, Yaroslavl Branch of the Memorial Society; Member, National Council, Memorial Society. Yaroslavl, December 14, 1990.

Marov, Viktor Fedorovich. Member, Architectural Planning Staff, Yaroslavl Region. Yaroslavl, December 13, 1990.

Maslennikov, Nikita Igor'evich. Advisor on Land Use, St. Petersburg City Soviet. Washington, D.C., (with Kaganova) October 22, 23, 1991; Washington, D.C., February 18, 1992; Baltimore, Md., October 2–5, 1992; Washington, D.C., February 9, 1993.

Mesian, Eduard Aleksandrovich. Chairman, Yaroslavl Division, USSR Union of Architects. Yaroslavl, October 11, 1991; Yaroslavl, September 2, 1992.

Mizulin, Mikhail Iur'evich. Director, Yaroslavl Regional Information and Data Center. Yaroslavl, April 16, 1993; Yaroslavl, September 9, 1993.

Mozeiko, Leonid Chisliavovich. Staff Member, Office for International Trade and Cooperation of the Yaroslavl Regional Executive Committee; President, Yartec Investment Firm. Yaroslavl, June 26, 1990; Yaroslavl, April 16, 1993.

Mozolin, Viktor Pavlovich. Section Chief, Institute of State and Law, USSR Academy of Sciences. Washington, D.C., October 31, 1990; Trento, Italy, April 9–11, 1991.

Nikolashchenko, Boris Vasil'evich. Chief, Scientific Research and Design Institute of the Master Plan for the Development of the City of St. Petersburg and Leningrad Region. St. Petersburg, September 13, 1991; Baltimore, Md., October 4, 1992.

Norkin, Kemer Borisovich. General Director, Department of the Mayor, Moscow Municipal Administration; Chair, Associational Council of Moscow City and Moscow Region. Moscow, September 13, 1993 (with Samoikin).

Okunkov, Lev Andreevich. Director, Institute of Legislation and Comparative Jurisprudence of the Russian Parliament. Moscow, September, 7, 1992; Moscow, April 21, 1993; Cambridge, Mass., October 29–30, 1993.

Ol'khovik, Gennadi Feodos'evich. Chairman, Commission on Science, Education, Culture, and Upbringing, Yaroslavl Regional Council. Yaroslavl, April 14, 1993.

Ometov, Boris Nikolaevich. Chairman, Department of State Inspection of Monument Protection (St. Petersburg). St. Petersburg, September 12–13, 1991; Baltimore, Md., October 2–4, 1992.

Peregudov, Father Mikhail Mikhailovich. Deputy, Yaroslavl Regional Soviet. Yaroslavl, June 25, 1990 (with Vasil'eva and Boborykin); Yaroslavl, December 13, 1990.

Polunin, Vladimir Ivanovich. Chair, Kiev District Council of the City of Moscow. Moscow, October 17, 1991.

Ponomarev, Dmitrii Zakharovich. Specialist, Regional Information-Analytical Administration, Yaroslavl Region. Yaroslavl, April 14, 1993 (with Bushuev).

Razlogov, Kiril Emil'evich. Director, Scientific Research Institute of Culture, USSR Ministry of Culture, Moscow. Washington, D.C., October 23, 1990; Moscow, December 16, 1990; Moscow, October 17, 1991; Washington, D.C., November 19, 1991; Moscow, August 25, 1992; Moscow, April 17, 1993; Washington, D.C., September 22–24, 1993.

Rumiantseva, Tatiana Pavlovna. Deputy Director, Yaroslavl Regional Executive Committee Public Opinion Research Center; Director, Sociological Center, Yaroslavl City Council; Director, Yaroslavl City Sociological Center attached to the Municipal Administration. Yaroslavl, June 19–27, 1990; Yaroslavl, December 10–15, 1990; Yaroslavl, October 10–16, 1991; Yaroslavl, April 26–29, 1992; Yaroslavl, August 31–September 4, 1992; Yaroslavl, April 15, 1993; Yaroslavl, September 6–10, 1993; Washington, D.C., November 9–13, 1993.

Samoikin, Iurii Mikhailovich. Deputy, Moscow City Soviet; Member, Moscow City Soviet Commission on Economic Activity; Deputy Chief, Moscow Division, Russian Federation State Committee for Anti-Monopoly Policy and Promotion of New Economic Structures. Moscow, July 2, 1990; Trento, Italy, January 18–19, 1991; Moscow, September 3, 13 (with Norkin), 1993.

Savinov, Aleksandr Germanovich. Deputy Chair, Committee on the Administration of Municipal Property, Yaroslavl City Mayor's Office. Yaroslavl, April 29, 1992 (with Vornarev).

Semenov, Evgenii Anatolivich. Organizer, Yaroslavl City Pioneer Palace. Yaroslavl, December 14, 1990.

Sevan, Olga Grigor'evna. Scientific Research Institute of Culture, Russian Federation Ministry of Culture, Moscow. Moscow, December 16, 1990; Washington, D.C., September 27–29, 1991; Moscow, October 17, 1991; Moscow, April 30, 1992; Moscow, August 25–28, 1992; Moscow, April 17, 1993.

Sevastianova, Alla Aleksandrovna. Professor of History, Yaroslavl State University. Yaroslavl, October 15, 1991; Washington, D.C., 1992; Yaroslavl, April 28, 1992 (with Kozliakov); Yaroslavl, April 13, 1993.

Shemenev, Valentin Nikolaevich. Director, Yaroslavl Regional Executive Committee Public Opinion Research Center. Yaroslavl, June 19–27, 1990; Yaroslavl, December 15–16, 1990.

Shvidkovskii, Dmitrii Olegovich. Architectural Historian, Moscow Architectural Institute. Moscow, April 20, 1993; Moscow, September 10, 1993.

Sokolova, Ksenia Aleksandrovna. Member, Architectural Planning Staff, Yaroslavl Regional Executive Committee. Yaroslavl, June 24, 1990.

Sulakshin, Stepan Stepanovich. Representative of the President of the Russian Federation in Tomsk. Washington, D.C., February 26, 1992; Washington, D.C., July 21, 1992; Washington, D.C., October 8, 1992.

Tikhomirov, Iurii Aleksandrovich. First Deputy Director, Institute of Legislation and Comparative Jurisprudence of the Russian Federation. Moscow, September 6, 1993.

Tikhonov, Lev Petrovich. Deputy Chairman, Russian Society for the Preservation of Monuments, St. Petersburg Branch. St. Petersburg, September 13, 1992; Baltimore, Md., October 2–4, 1992.

Timonin, Valerii Leonidovich. Staff Member, Foreign Trade Department, Yaroslavl Motor Works; Lay Leader, Orthodox Church. Yaroslavl, December 14, 1990.

Ul'ianov, Oleg Germanovich. Chief, Archaeological Sector, Central Museum of Ancient Russian Culture and Arts. Moscow, August 25, 1992; Moscow, April 20, 1993.

Varukhin, Vladimir Gennad'evich. Representative of the President of Russia to Yaroslavl. Yaroslavl, October 11, 1991.

Vasil'eva, Tatiana L'vovna. Director, Yaroslavl Regional Administration for Preservation of Historic Monuments. Yaroslavl, June 25, 1990 (with Boborykin and Peregudov); Yaroslavl, December 11, 1990; Yaroslavl, September 3, 1992.

Verbitskii, Iurii Ivanovich. Deputy, Yaroslavl City Soviet; Chair, Commission on Culture of the Yaroslavl City Soviet; Chair, Independent City Commission on the Privatization of the Housing Fund; Chief, Department for the Organization of the Reconstruction of Historic Structures, Yaroslavl Municipal Administration. Yaroslavl, October 15, 1991; Yaroslavl, April 27–28, 1992; Yaroslavl, September 1–2, 1992; Yaroslavl, April 14, 1993; Yaroslavl, September 7, 1993.

Veselov, Aleksandr Nikolaevich. Chairman, Yaroslavl Regional Soviet. Yaroslavl, June 19, 1990 (with Kolbatskii); Yaroslavl, October 11, 1991; Yaroslavl, September 1, 1992.

Vinnichenko, Valentin Alekseevich. Director, Yaroslavl City Executive Committee Center for Public Opinion Research. Yaroslavl, June 22, 1990 (with Kuznetsov).

Vinogradov, Viktor Alekseevich. Chief Architect, Izmailovo Restoration Center, Moscow. Moscow, August 28, 1992.

Volonchunas, Viktor Vladimirovich. Mayor, Yaroslavl. Yaroslavl, April 27, 1992; Washington, D.C., April 7, 1993.

Vornarev, Aleksandr Vasil'evich. Chair, Fund of Municipal Property, Yaroslavl City Soviet. Yaroslavl, April 29, 1992 (with Savinov); Yaroslavl, September 1, 1992; Yaroslavl, April 13, 1993.

Voronin, Nikolai Pavlovich. Secretary for Ideology, Yaroslavl Regional Communist Party Committee. Yaroslavl, June 19, 1990.

Vysokovskii, Aleksandr Arkad'evich. Department Head, All-Union Scientific

Research Institute of the Theory of Architecture and City Planning; President, Russian Association of Urbanists; Director, "Polis-3" Consulting Firm. Moscow, July, 1, 1990; Moscow, December 16, 1990; Moscow, October 8, 1991; Moscow, April 25, May 2, 1992; Moscow, April 11, 18, 1993; Moscow, September 11, 1993.

Yankov, Kirill Vadimovich. Chairman of the Economic Reform Committee, Moscow Regional Council of People's Deputies. Washington, D.C., February 24, 1993; Washington, D.C., April 6, 1993.

Zelinskaia, Elena. Member, Leningrad People's Front; Press Secretary for Leningrad City Soviet. Leningrad, January 23, 1990; Washington, D.C., May 14, 1990.

Zharikov, Viktor Mikhailovich. Director, Department of Foreign Economic Activities, Yaroslavl Regional Administration. Yaroslavl, September 7, 8 (with Bykov), 1993.

Zheltyakov, Vasilii Tikhonovich. Chief Engineer, Yaroslavl Motor Works Avtodizel'. Yaroslavl, April 29, 1992 (with Chervnikov).

Zlobin, Nikolai Vasil'evich. Professor, Moscow State University. Washington, D.C., January 4, 1992.

BOOKS, ARTICLES, AND PAPERS

Apal'kov, Sergei. "Vsem tserkvam tserkov'. . . ." *Spasenie,* May 17–18, 1992, p. 7.

Bater, James H. *The Soviet City: Ideal and Reality.* London: Edward Arnold, 1980.

Bekker, Aleksandr, "Iaroslavl' ishchet mesto v zhizni," *Segodnia,* July 6, 1993, p. 3.

Beliakov, Sergei. "Iulis Kolbovskii: 'Vse chto mozhno bylo, ia delal.' " *Iunost'* (Yaroslavl), October 16, 1993, p. 1.

Berezneva, Elena. "Vse khotiat delit'. Kto budet stroit'?" *Kommersant,* April 19, 1991, p. 1.

Bestor, Theodore C. "Visible Hands: Auctions and Institutional Integration in the Tsukiji Wholesale Fish Market, Tokyo." Unpublished paper prepared for discussion by the Economic Sociology Workshop Group, Russell Sage Foundation, New York City, June 12, 1992.

Bohlen, Celestine. "Yeltsin Promotes a Charter That Is Very Much His." *New York Times,* November 10, 1993, p. A18.

Bolotseva, I. P. "Ch'i na rusi ikony?" *Vash vybor,* 1993, no. 1 (January): 43.

———. "Il'ya Prorok: sud'ba i vremia." *Severnyi rabochii,* July 15, 1990, p. 3.

Bonet, Pilar. *Figures in a Red Landscape.* Translated by Norman Thomas di Giovanni and Susan Ashe. Washington, D.C.: Woodrow Wilson Center Press; Baltimore: Johns Hopkins University Press, 1993.

Boyce, Nani Kulish. "Housing in St. Petersburg, Russia: From a Centrally-Planned System to the Western-Market Orientation." Unpublished manuscript prepared at the Urban Transportation Center, University of Illinois at Chicago, May 8, 1992.

———. "Russia on the Way to a Housing Market: A Case Study of St. Petersburg." *Environment and Planning Annual* (Great Britain) 25 (1993): 975–86.

Boyer, M. Christine. "Cities for Sale: Merchandising History at South Street Seaport." In Michael Sorkin, ed., *Variations on a Theme Park: The New American City and the End of Public Space,* pp. 181–204. New York: Hill and Wang/Noonday Press, 1992.

Braunfels, Wolfgang. *Urban Design in Western Europe: Regime and Architecture, 900–1900.* Translated by Kenneth J. Northcott. Chicago: University of Chicago Press, 1988.

Brumfield, William Craft. *A History of Russian Architecture.* Cambridge: Cambridge University Press, 1993.

———. *Lost Russia: Photographing the Ruins of Russian Architecture.* Durham, N.C.: Duke University Press, forthcoming.

———, ed. *Reshaping Russian Architecture: Western Technology, Utopian Dreams.* Cambridge: Cambridge University Press, 1990.

Brumfield, William Craft, and Blair A. Ruble, eds. *Russian Housing in the Modern Age: Design and Social History.* Cambridge: Cambridge University Press; Washington, D.C.: Woodrow Wilson Center Press, 1993.

Burgel, Guy. *La Ville Aujourd'hui.* Paris: Hachette, 1993.

Bush, Keith. "Enterprise Privatization Decree." *RFE/RL Daily Report,* no. 244 (December 30, 1991): 2.

———. "Land Privatization Decree." *RFE/RL Daily Report,* no. 244 (December 30, 1991): 2.

———. "Popov's Plans for Moscow." *RFE/RL Daily Report,* no. 179 (September 19, 1991: 1.

———. "Privatization in Russia." *RFE/RL Daily Report,* no. 1 (January 2, 1992): 2.

———. "Progress of Russian Privatization." *RFE/RL Daily Report,* no. 1 (January 4, 1993): 1.

———. "Russian Privatization Program Approved." *RFE/RL Daily Report,* no. 243 (December 27, 1991): 2.

Cromley, E. C. *Alone Together: A History of New York's Early Apartments.* Ithaca, N.Y.: Cornell University Press, 1990.

Custine, Marquis de (Astolphe Louis Leonor). *Russia: Translated from the French of the Marquis de Custine.* New York: D. Appleton, 1854.

Davydova, Natalia. "Vse blizhe, i blizhe, i blizhe." *Moskovskie novosti,* no. 16 (April 21, 1991): 4.

DiMaio, A. J. *Soviet Urban Housing: Problems and Policies.* New York: Praeger, 1974.

Dobbs, Michael. "In Yaroslavl, Perestroika Brings Only More Hardship." *Washington Post,* November 7, 1989, pp. Al, A20.

Dychinskii, A. Ts. "Chelovek i sreda obitaniia." *S.-Peterburgskaia panorama,* 1992, no. 9: 26–29.

Erlanger, Steve. "In St. Petersburg, a Fight over Power and Property." *New York Times,* April 27, 1992, p. A3.

"Eshche odin fond. . . ." *Gorodskie novosti,* September 3–9, 1992, p. 2.

Fabrichnikova, Larisa. "Dazhe rzhavogo gvozdia ne ostavili." *Zolotoe kol'tso,* October 8, 1993, p. 4.

Feshbach, Murray, and Alfred Friendly, Jr. *Ecocide in the USSR.* New York: Basic Books, 1992.

Fishman, Robert. "Megalopolis Unbound." *Wilson Quarterly* 14 (1990): 25–45.

"Fond munitsipal'nogo imushchestva g. Iaroslavlia ob"iavliaet torgi na 20 avgusta 1992 sleduiushchikh predpriiatii." *Gorodskie novosti,* July 23, 1992, p. 2.

"Fond munitsipal'nogo imushchestva g. Iaroslavlia ob"iavliaet torgi na 29 sentiabria." *Gorodskie novosti,* August 27, 1992, p. 4.

French, R. A. "Conserving the Past in Soviet Cities." *Kennan Institute Occa-*

sional Paper No. 235. Washington, D.C.: Kennan Institute for Advanced Russian Studies/Woodrow Wilson International Center for Scholars, 1990.

French, R. A., and F. E. Ian Hamilton, eds. *The Socialist City: Spatial Structure and Urban Policy.* New York: John Wiley and Sons, 1979.

Garreau, Joel. *Edge City: Life on the New Frontier.* New York: Doubleday, 1991.

Gel'man, Vladimir, and Mary McAuley. "The Politics of City Government: Leningrad/St. Petersburg." In Jeffrey W. Hahn and Theodore Friedgut, eds., *Local Power and Post-Soviet Politics.* Armonk, N.Y.: M. E. Sharpe, 1994, pp. 15–42.

"General'nyi plan razvitiia Leningrada." In Planovaia komissiia ispolkoma Lengorsoveta, Statisticheskoe upravlenie goroda Leningrada, *Leningrad za 50 let: Statisticheskii sbornik.* Leningrad: Lenizdat, 1967.

Glazer, Nathan. "The Prince, the People, and the Architects." *American Scholar* 59 (Autumn 1990): 505–18.

Glazychev, Vyacheslav. "Malyi gorod. Tekhnologiia vyzhivaniia i razvitiia." *Svobodnaia mysl',* 1993, no. 7: 9–18.

———. "Social Change in Provincial Russian Towns." Seminar presentation at the Kennan Institute for Advanced Russian Studies, Washington, D.C., May 10, 1993.

Glukhov, K. A. *Privatizatsiia zhil'ia (kommentarii k zakonodatel'stvu).* Moscow: Iuridicheskaia firma "Paritet," MGU im. M. V. Lomonosova, 1991.

Goode, James M. *Best Addresses: A Century of Washington's Distinguished Apartment Houses.* Washington, D.C.: Smithsonian Institution Press, 1988.

Gorobchenko, T. "Nakanune otkrytiia." *Severnyi krai,* September 11, 1993, p. 2.

Goskomstat RSFSR, Iaroslavskii gorodskoi otdel statistiki. *Statisticheskii biulleten'. Dannye o zhilishchnom fonde goroda Iaroslavlia za 1989 god.* Iaroslavl': Goskomstat RSFSR, Iaroslavskii Otdel, February 1990.

Grigor'ev, V. "Kruglyi stol 'SP': Zapovednik Peterburgskoi kul'tury." *S.-Peterburgskaia panorama,* 1992, no. 3: 17–19.

Gumbel, Peter. "Soviet Elections Promise Big Changes." *Wall Street Journal,* February 23, 1990, p. A8.

Hahn, Jeffrey W. "The Evolution of Local Legislatures: The Case of Yaroslavl'." Paper presented at the conference "Democratization in Russia: The Development of Legislative Institutions," Harvard University, Cambridge, Mass., October 29–30, 1993.

———. "Local Politics and Political Power in Russia: The Case of Yaroslavl'." *Soviet Economy* 7, no. 4 (1991): 322–41.

Hahn, Jeffrey W., and Theodore Friedgut, eds. *Local Power and Post-Soviet Politics.* Armonk, N.Y.: M. E. Sharpe, 1994.

Hahn, Jeffrey W., and Gavin Helf. "Old Dogs and New Tricks: Party Elites in the Russian Regional Elections of 1990." *Slavic Review* 51, no. 3 (Fall 1992): 511–30.

Hamilton, Ellen. "Social Areas under State Socialism: The Case of Moscow." In Susan Gross Solomon, ed., *Beyond Sovietology: Essays in Politics and History,* pp. 192–225. Armonk, N.Y.: M. E. Sharpe, 1993.

Hanson, Charles, Nadezhda Kosareva, and Raymond Struyk. "Housing Reform in the Russian Federation: A Review of Three Cities and Their Transition to a Market Economy." In *Urban Institute International Activities Center Research Paper,* pp. 1–2. Washington, D.C.: Urban Institute, 1992.

Hanson, Charles, and Raymond Struyk. "USAID Technical Assistance Strategy for the Russian Federation in the Shelter Sector." In *Urban Institute International Activities Center Research Paper*, pp. 9–10. Washington, D.C.: Urban Institute, 1992.

Hanson, Philip. "Housing Problems." *RFE/RL Daily Report*, no. 129 (July 10, 1991): 7.

Hardoy, Jorge E., and Margarita Gutman. "The Role of Municipal Government in the Protection of Historic Centres in Latin American Cities." *Environment and Urbanization* 3, no. 1 (April 1991): 96–108.

Hawes, Elizabeth. *New York, New York: How the Apartment House Transformed the Life of the City (1869–1930)*. New York: Alfred A. Knopf, 1993.

Hiatt, Fred. "Yeltsin Launches Plan to Spur Private Land Ownership." *Washington Post*, October 27, 1993, p. A27.

———. "Yeltsin to Let Foreigners Buy Russian Land." *Washington Post*, June 13, 1992, p. A15.

Hough, Jerry F. *The Soviet Prefects: The Local Party Organs in Industrial Decision-Making*. Cambridge, Mass.: Harvard University Press, 1969.

Hough, Jerry F., and Merle Fainsod. *How the Soviet Union Is Governed*. Cambridge, Mass.: Harvard University Press, 1979.

IA 'Severo-Zapad'. "Itogi privatizatsii v Peterburge." *Nezavisimaia gazeta*, December 15, 1992, p. 4.

———. "Muzhiki ne ishchut kompromissa." *Nezavisimaia gazeta*, January 30, 1993, p. 6.

Imse, Ann. "A Housing Boom Remakes the Russian Landscape." *New York Times*, August 29, 1993, p. F5.

Jonas, Andrew E. G. "A Place for Politics in Urban Theory: The Organization and Strategies of Urban Coalitions." *Urban Geography* 13, no. 3 (1993): 280–90.

Kadibur, T. S. "Zhilishchnye usloviia naseleniia Sankt-Peterburga." In E. A. Poleshchuk and V. M. Makosii, eds., *Sankt-Peterburg v zerkale statistiki*, pp. 12–22. Sankt-Peterburg: Izdatel'stvo Sankt-Peterburgskogo universiteta ekonomiki i finansov, 1993.

Kaganova, O. Z. "Creating an Urban Real Estate Market in Russia." *Real Estate Issues* 18, no. 1 (Spring/Summer 1993): 45–48.

———. "One-Family Housing Allotment: Legal Guarantee, Present Status in St. Petersburg and in the Region, Draft of Reforms and Analysis." Report prepared for the Urban Institute, Washington, D.C., January-March 1992.

Kamenskii, V. A. "Itogi desiatiletnogo perioda realizatsii general'nogo plana razvitiia Leningrada utverzhdennogo Sovetom Ministrov SSSR v iiule 1966 goda." *Stroitel'stvo i arkhitektura Leningrada*, 1966, no. 7: 1–47.

———. *Leningrad. General'nyi plan razvitiia goroda*. Leningrad: Lenizdat, 1972.

Kantor, Paul, and H. V. Savitch. "Can Politicians Bargain with Business?: A Theoretical and Comparative Perspective on Urban Development." *Urban Affairs Quarterly*, December 1993.

———. "Urban Mobilization of Private Capital: A Cross-national Comparison." *Woodrow Wilson Center Comparative Urban Studies Occasional Paper Series, No. 3*. Washington, D.C.: Woodrow Wilson International Center for Scholars, 1993.

Karaseva, L. "Liudi vo chto-to veriat. . . ." *Severnyi rabochii,* August 9, 1990, p. 3.

Kazutin, Dmitry. "Rumours and Newspapers." *Moscow News Weekly,* 1990, no. 19: 5.

Khotchinskii, S. "Puti realizatsii stroitel'noi programmy." *Arkhitektura i stroitel'stvo Moskvy,* no. 5 (1957): 10–13.

Khrapchenko, V. "Stranitsy istorii: Vstrecha so 'skazaniem o postroenii grada Iaroslavlia." *Severnyi krai,* October 23, 1993, p. 1.

———. "V gostiakh u 'Sysoia'." *Severnyi krai,* October 13, 1993, p. 2.

Khrupalova, I. "Koridori vlasti: NaSovetovalis'?. . . ." *Severnyi krai,* October 27, 1993, pp. 1, 3.

Khrushchev, Nikita. *Khrushchev Remembers: The Last Testament.* Translated and edited by Strobe Talbott. Boston: Little, Brown, and Company, 1974.

Kibirev, S. "Arkhitektura i tipizatsiia massovogo zhilishchnogo stroitel'stva." *Arkhitektura SSSR,* 1968, no. 4: 20–24.

Kochurov, B. I. "Rossiia vo mgle. Ekologicheskii kommentarii." *Vash vybor,* 1993, no. 2 (February): 42–43.

Kolotilkin, B. "Perspektivy ispol'zovaniia piatietazhnykh zhilykh zdanii." *Arkhitektura SSSR,* 1979, no. 8: 16–17.

Kopylova, I. "27.10.93g. 10 chas. 07 min.: sovetskaia vlast' v Iaroslavle prekratila techenie svoe (pochti po Saltykovu-Shchedrinu)." *Severnyi krai,* October 29, 1993, p. 1.

Kornai, Janos. *Economics of Shortage.* Amsterdam: North-Holland, 1980.

———. " 'Hard' and 'Soft' Budget Constraints." *Acta Oeconomica* 25, nos. 3–4 (1980): 231–46.

Kostandi, M. "Osobennosti planirovki malometrazhnykh kvartir." *Arkhitektura SSSR,* no. 6 (1956): 10–14.

Kotkin, Stephen. "Shelter and Subjectivity in the Stalin Period: A Case Study of Magnitogorsk." In William Craft Brumfield and Blair A. Ruble, eds., *Russian Housing in the Modern Age: Design and Social History,* pp. 171–210. Cambridge: Cambridge University Press, 1993.

Kozliakov, Viacheslav. "Kogo strashil kolokol'nyi zvon?" *Iunost'* (Yaroslavl), May 20, 1989, p. 10.

———. "Vozvrashchaias k napechatannomu. Novye demonstratsii ne nuzhny!" *Iunost'* (Yaroslavl), June 16, 1987, p. 3.

Kozlov, L. I., and V. F. Marov. *Iaroslavl'. Putevoditel'-spravochnik.* Iaroslavl': Verkhne-volzhskoe knizhnoe izdatel'stvo, 1988.

Kubenko, G. D. "Komu ukroshchat' 'kovarnyi styk?" *Leningradskaia panorama,* no. 7 (1987): 39–40.

Kuz'michev, Andrei, and Igor' Shapkin. "Delovoi Iaroslavl'." *Vash vybor,* 1993, no. 1:18–21.

Lisitsyn, Anatolii. "Ne nado boiat'sia delit' polnomochiia." *Vash vybor,* 1992, no. 11 (November): 6–7.

———. "Obrashchenie A. I. Lisitsyna." *Severnyi krai,* October 5, 1993, p. 1.

Lisitsyn, Anatolii, Sergei Burov, Aleksei Bushuev, Evgenii Golubev, Dmitrii Maksimov, Aleksandr Miklin, Dmitrii Ponomarev, and Il'ia Skorokhovod. "Regional'naia politika: opyt i printsipy." *Vash vybor,* 1993, no. 1 (January): 34–35.

Lisovskii, Vladimir. "Spasti i sokhranit'." *S.-Peterburgskaia panorama* 1992, no. 4: 28–30.

Lowenthal, David. *The Past Is a Foreign Country.* Cambridge: Cambridge University Press, 1985.

Loyer, Françoise. *Paris Nineteenth Century: Architecture and Urbanism.* Translated by Charles Lyon Clark. New York: Abbeville Press, 1988.

Lynch, Kevin. *The Image of the City.* Cambridge, Mass.: MIT Press, 1959.

Malinina, N. A., and Iu. A. Iakovleva. "Rossiiskii rynok zhil'ia." *S.-Peterburgskaia panorama,* 1992, no. 7: 7.

Marnie, Sheila. "Land Reform in Russia." *RFE/RL Daily Report,* no. 1 (January 4, 1993): 1.

———. "Privatization of Housing." *RFE/RL Daily Report,* no. 218 (November 11, 1992): 2.

———. "Russian Parliament Approves Land Legislation." *RFE/RL Daily Report,* no. 138 (July 22, 1993): 2.

Mel'nikov, P. I. (Andrei Perchinskii). *V lesakh.* Moscow, 1871–74.

Mendras, Marie. "Les Trois Russies: Analyse du referendum du 25 avril 1993." *Revue Française de Science Politique* 43, no. 6 (December 1993): 897–939.

Mezhevich, M. N. "Upravlenie razvitiem gorodov: potrebnosti i real'nosti." In P. N. Lebedev and V. S. Sukhin, eds., *Chelovek i obshchestvo no. 16: Sotsial'nye problemy planirovaniia sotsialisticheskogo goroda,* pp. 54–55. Leningrad: LGU-NIIKSI, 1977.

Mitchneck, Beth. "The Changing Role of the Local Budget in Russian Cities: The Case of Yaroslavl'." In Jeffrey W. Hahn and Theodore Friedgut, eds., *Local Power and Post-Soviet Politics.* Armonk, N.Y.: M. E. Sharpe, 1994.

———. "The Local Budget in the Changing Role of Municipal Government in Russia: A Case Study of Iaroslavl'." *Report of the National Council for Soviet and East European Research.* 1993.

Mnatsakanian, Ruben A. *Environmental Legacy of the Former Soviet Republics (as Collated from Official Statistics).* Edinburgh: Centre for Human Ecology, University of Edinburgh, 1992.

Moiseev, Vladimir. "Istoriia ZhSK mozhet zavershit'sia v Rossii." *Nezavisimaia gazeta,* January 11, 1993, p. 6.

Mollenkopf, John Hall. *The Contested City.* Princeton: Princeton University Press, 1983.

———. *A Phoenix in the Ashes: The Rise and Fall of the Koch Coalition in New York City Politics.* Princeton: Princeton University Press, 1992.

Morton, Henry W. "Housing in the Soviet Union." *Academy of Political Science Proceedings* 35, no. 3 (1984).

———. "Who Gets What, When, and How? Housing in the Soviet Union." *Soviet Studies* 31, no. 2 (1980): 235–59.

Narodnoe khoziaistvo Leningrada i Leningradskoi oblasti v desiatoi piatiletke: Statisticheskii sbornik. Leningrad: Lenizdat, 1981.

Nefedova, Tat'iana. "Iaroslavskoe selo." *Vash vybor,* 1993, no. 1 (January): 10–11.

Nelson, Lynn, Lilia V. Babaeva, and Rufat O. Babaev. "Perspectives on Entrepreneurship and Privatization in Russia: Policy and Public Opinion." *Slavic Review* 51, no. 2 (Summer 1992): 270–86.

Nelson, Lynn D., and Irina Y. Kuzes. *Property to the People: The Struggle for Radical Economic Reform in Russia.* Armonk, N.Y.: M. E. Sharpe, 1994.

Nevinnaia, I. "Osobniaki budut u bogatykh." *Trud,* August 28, 1992, p. 3.

Nichemias, Carol. "The Impact of Soviet Housing Policy on Housing Conditions in Soviet Cities: The Uneven Push from Moscow." *Urban Studies* 18, no. 1 (February 1981): 1–8.

Nikitin, Pavel. "Iaroslavskii barometr." *Ogonek*, 1990, no. 26: 9–11.

Norton, Thomas E., and Jerry E. Petterson. *Living It Up: A Guide to the Named Apartment Houses of New York*. New York: Atheneum, 1984.

" 'Novaia Golandiia'. Kakoi ei byt?" *S.-Peterburgskaia panorama*, 1992, no. 4: 18–19.

Olenik, Nikolai. "Problema peredachi khramov ne imeet prostykh reshenii." *Nezavisimaia gazeta*, January 6, 1993, p. 5.

Pallot, Judith, and Denis J. B. Shaw. *Planning in the Soviet Union*. Athens: University of Georgia Press, 1981.

Pavlova, Irina, "Strannopriimnyi dom na Rostovskom trakte." *Vash vybor*, 1993, no. 1 (January): 22–23.

Peterson, D. J. *Troubled Lands: The Legacy of Soviet Environmental Destruction*. Boulder, Colo.: Westview Press, 1993.

Pokhmelkin, Andrei, and Viktor Pokhmelkin. "Zakon protiv traditsii." *Vash vybor*, 1992, no. 11: 8–10.

Poleshchuk, E. A., and V. M. Makosii, eds. *Sankt-Peterburg v zerkale statistiki*. Sankt-Peterburg: Izdatel'stvo Sankt-Peterburgskogo universiteta ekonomiki i finansov, 1993.

Polukeev, Oleg. "Velikaia zemel'naia reforma?" *Nezavisimaia gazeta*, October 29, 1993, p. 1.

"Pravil'no, nauchno reshat' problemy tipizatsii zhilykh domov." *Arkhitektura SSSR*, 1956, no. 5: 1–4.

Pushkarnaia, A. "Frantsuzskii dom v rossiiskom inter'ere." *Severnyi krai*, September 11, 1993, p. 1.

———. "Iaroslavskii malyi gorsovet: segodnia my znaem, kto est' kto." *Severnyi krai*, October 30, 1993, p. 1.

Putnam, Robert. *Making Democracy Work: Civic Tradition in Modern Italy*. Princeton: Princeton University Press, 1993.

Raban, Jonathan. *Soft City*. London: Harvill/HarperCollins, 1988.

Renaud, Bertrand. "The Housing System in the Former Soviet Union: Why the Soviets Need Housing Markets." *Housing Policy Debate*, 1992, vol. 3, no. 3, pp. 877–99.

Rodin, Ivan. "Sovetskaia predstavitel'naia vlast' polnost'iu likvidirovana." *Nezavisimaia gazeta*, October 28, 1993, p. 1.

———. "Vitsemer nedovolen birzhei nedvizhimosti." *Nezavisimaia gazeta*, May 16, 1992, p. 6.

Ruble, Blair A. "From *Khrushcheby* to *Korobki*: Domesticity Returns." In William Craft Brumfield and Blair A. Ruble, eds., *Russian Housing in the Modern Age: Design and Social History*, pp. 232–70. Cambridge: Cambridge University Press, 1993.

———. *Leningrad: Shaping a Soviet City*. Berkeley: University of California Press, 1990.

———. "Novyi oblik goroda: politika sobstvennosti v Iaroslavle." In Iaroslavskii gorodskoi sovet narodnykh deputatov i Tsentr izucheniia obshchestvennogo mneniia i sotsiologicheskikh issledovanii "TsIOMSI," *Mezhdunarodnaia nauchno-prakticheskaia konferentsiia: Predstavitel'nye organy mestnogo samoupravleniia v sovremennom mire. Doklady. Tezisy vystuplenii, materialy diskussii (27–28 aprelia 1992 goda)*, pp. 95–125. Iaroslavl': Iaroslavskii gorodskoi sovet narodnykh deputatov, 1993.

————. "Policy Innovation and the Soviet Political Process: The Case of Socio-economic Planning in Leningrad." *Canadian Slavonic Papers* 24, no. 2 (June 1982): 161–74.

————. "Reshaping the City: The Politics of Property in a Provincial Russian City." *Urban Anthology* 21, no. 3 (1992): 203–33.

Rybakov, Andrei. "Sud'ba sobstvennosti, kak sobstvennaia sud'ba." *Vash vybor,* 1993, no. 1 (January): 14–16.

Safronov, Sergei. "V kogo veriat Iaroslavtsy." *Vash vybor,* 1993, no. 2 (February): 28–29.

Savinova, N. A., and T. V. Iurepina, eds. *Privatizatsiia. Polnyi paket dokumentov.* Moscow: Rossiiskoe pravo, 1992.

Sdobnov, Iu., E. Rozhanov, and A. Ikonnikov. "Iaroslavl'. Tri tochki zreniia na problemu svoeobraziia." *Arkhitektura SSSR,* 1981, no. 9: 16–21.

"Segodnia—otkrytie pamiatnika Iaroslavu Mudromu." *Severnyi krai,* October 23, 1993, p. 1.

Sevast'ianova, Alla. "Nuzhna pravovaia osnova." *Severnyi rabochii,* August 9, 1990, p. 3.

Sevriukov, D. "Zhit', kak v shtatakh." *Zolotoe kol'tso,* August 13, 1992, p. 1.

Sevriukov, Iu. "Mister Dikkens iz Radforda." *Severnyi krai,* August 8, 1992, p. 2.

Shaw, Denis J. B. "Planning Leningrad." *Geographical Review* 68, no. 2 (April 1978): 189.

"Shire razvertyvat' zhilishchnoe stroitel'stvo." *Arkhitektura SSSR,* 1956, no. 10: 29–30.

Skladchikov, Dmitrii. "Pervyi auktsion kvartir v Moskve: million za rublevki." *Kommersant,* April 22–29, 1991, p. 5.

Solomon, Susan Gross, ed. *Beyond Sovietology: Essays in Politics and History.* Armonk, N.Y.: M. E. Sharpe, 1993.

Stoner-Weiss, Kathryn. "Local Heroes: Political Exchange and Regional Government Performance in Post-Communist Russia." Ph.D. diss., Harvard University, Cambridge, Mass., 1994.

Struyk, Raymond J., Nadezhda Kosareva, Jennifer Daniell, Charles Hanson, and Maris Mikelsons. *Implementing Housing Allowances in Russia: Rationalizing the Rental Sector.* Washington, D.C.: Urban Institute, 1993.

Sudjic, Deyan. *The 100 Mile City.* San Diego: Harcourt Brace, 1992.

Suttles, Gerald D. *The Man-made City: The Land-Use Confidence Game in Chicago.* Chicago: University of Chicago Press, 1990.

Tanaka, Stefan. *Japan's Orient: Rendering Pasts into History.* Berkeley: University of California Press, 1993.

Treivish, Andrei. "Tipichnyi krizis v tipichnom regione." *Vash vybor,* 1993, no. 1: 12–13.

Trushchenko, O. E. "Akkumuliatsiia simvolicheskogo kapitala v prostranstve stolichnogo tsentra." *Rossiiskii monitor* 3 (1993): 145–65.

Tsvetkov, Aleksandr. "Prikliucheniia frantsuzov v gostinitse 'Kotorosl'." *Zolotoe kol'tso,* October 6, 1993, p. 1.

Turchenko, S. "Grimasy Armeisko depolizatsii. Porno v trapeznoi." *Sovetskaia Rossiia,* April 6, 1993, p. 4.

Uchitelle, Louis. "Now All Moscow Apartments Have a View." *New York Times,* February 28, 1992, p. A10.

Urmanov, Alexander. "The Creeping Counterrevolution in Russia: Local Resistance to Privatization." *Heritage Foundation Backgrounder,* no. 879 (February 6, 1992): 5.

"V oblastnoi administratsii: 'Feniks'—eshche ne sinitsa v ruke. No i ne zhuravl' v nebe." *Severnyi krai,* October 27, 1993, p. 1.

Vaganova, I. "Bor'ba za pamiatniki byla nachalom politicheskikh strastei." *Zolotoe kol'tso,* August 15, 1992, p. 4.

Veselov, A. N. "Obrashchenie A. N. Veselova." *Severnyi krai,* October 5, 1993, p. 1.

Volkov, Dmitrii. "Moszhiluchet budet prodavat' kvartiry s auktsiona." *Kommersant,* February 18–25, 1991, p. 4.

"Vsemerno uluchshat' tipovye proekty povyshat' kachestvo massovogo zhilishnogo stroitel'stva v SSSR (Postanovlenie. 31 iiulia 1957 g.)." *Arkhitektura SSSR,* 1957, no. 10: 29–30.

Vysokovskii, Aleksandr. "Will Domesticity Return?" In William Craft Brumfield and Blair A. Ruble, eds., *Russian Housing in the Modern Age: Design and Social History,* pp. 271–308. Cambridge: Cambridge University Press, 1993.

Whitney, Craig R. "Yeltsin Appears in Public to Honor a Hero of the Past." *New York Times,* October 24, 1993, p. 12.

Wilson, Elizabeth. *The Sphinx in the City: Urban Life, the Control of Disorder, and Women.* Berkeley: University of California Press, 1992.

Wood, Ruth Kedzie. *Honeymooning in Russia.* New York: Dodd, Mead, 1911.

Yeremicheva, Galina, and Nani Kulish Boyce. "Privatization of Housing in St. Petersburg, Russia." *Environment and Planning Annual* (Great Britain) 24 (1992): 177–80.

Zaslavsky, Ilya N. "Population Geography and Settlement Planning in the USSR." *Planning Theory Newsletter* (Milano), nos. 5–6 (1991): 179–87.

Zavarikhin, S. P. "Progulka po prospektu prosveshcheniia." *Leningradskaia panorama,* 1986, no. 9: 20–23.

STATUTES, DECREES, AND LEGAL DOCUMENTS

Glava administratsii Iaroslavskoi oblasti. "Postanovlenie No. 273, 27.10.93 'O reforme organa predstavitel'noi vlasti Iaroslavskoi oblasti'." *Severnyi krai,* October 30, 1993, p. 1.

Iaroslavskii gorodskoii ispolnitel'yii komitet. "Iaroslavl'. Skhema goroda: ekonomicheskoe zonirovanie territorii." 1991.

Iaroslavskii gorodskoi sovet narodnykh deputatov, Shestaia sessiia dvadtsat' pervogo sozyva. "Reshenie ot 25.06.91 o merakh po obespecheniiu ekonomiko-pravogo regulirovaniia pol'zovaniia zemel'nymi resursami g. Iaroslavlia." June 25, 1991.

"Iz protokola No. 65 schetnoi komissii o poimennom golosovanii po voprosu o predstavlenii prokurora oblasti O. A. Fisuna o dache soglasiia na privlechenie k ugolognoi otvetstvennosti deputata Nefedova, V. N." *Zolotoe kol'tso,* March 26, 1993, p. 3.

"Law of the RSFSR on Privatization of State and Municipal Enterprises." *Moscow Business Week,* no. 12 (June 4, 1992): 7–10.

Malyi sovet Iaroslavskogo gorodskogo soveta narodnykh deputatov. "Polozhenie o nezavisimoi komissii po privatizatsii zhilishchnogo fonda v gorode Iaroslavle." May 6, 1992.

———. "Polozhenie o poriadke privatizatsii munitsipal'nykh predpriiatii i imushchestva g. Iaroslavlia.'" 1991.

———. "Programma-Zadanie na razrabotku general'nogo plana g. Iaroslavlia, utverzhddanno Predsedatelem ispolkoma Iaroslavskogo gorodskogo Soveta narodnykh deputatov i TsNIIP gradostritel'stva." Iaroslavl', 1990.

———. "Reshenie No. 4 o poriadke doizbraniia malogo soveta gorodskogo soveta narodykh deputatov." January 23, 1992.

———. "Reshenie No. 5 o meropriiatiiakh po uluchsheniiu ekologicheskogo sostoianiia pochv g. Iaroslavlia i prigorodnykh territorii." January 23, 1992.

———. "Reshenie No. 12 o poriadke osushchestvleniia kontrolia za ispol'zovaniem i okhranoi zemel' v g. Iaroslavlia." January 23, 1992.

———. "Reshenie No. 13 o zapreshchenii snos starykh zdanii i sooruzhenii v zonakh okhrany i regulirovanii zastroiki g. Iaroslavlia." February 5, 1992.

———. "Reshenie No. 20 o privatizatsii munitsipal'nykh predpriiatii i imushchestva g. Iaroslavlia na 1992 god." February 13, 1992.

———. "Reshenie No. 41 o provedenii inventarizatsii zemli i stroenii i utverzhenii stavok zemel'nogo naloga na territorii g. Iaroslavlia." March 18, 1992.

———. "Reshenie No. 65 o vnesenii dopolnenii i izmenenii v polozhenie o poriadke i usloviiakh privatizatsii zhilishchnogo fonda v gorode Iaroslavl." April 8, 1992.

———. "Reshenie No. 72 Malogo soveta i Postanovlenie Mera goroda No. 384 o rassmotrenii zemel'nykh sporov na territorii g. Iaroslavlia." April 29, 1992.

———. "Reshenie No. 75 o vnesenii izmenenii i dopolnenii v reshenie malogo soveta No. 20 ot 13.02.92 g. o privatizatsii munitsipal'nykh predpriiatii i imushchestva g. Iaroslavlia." April 29, 1992.

———. "Reshenie No. 87 o predsedatele nezavisimoi komissii po privatizatsii zhil'ia." April 22, 1992.

———. "Reshenie No. 94 o sozdanii gorodskoi nezavisimoi komissii po privatizatsii zhilishchnogo fonda v gorode Iaroslavle." May 6, 1992.

———. "Spravka ob ekologicheskom sostoianii pochv g. Iarolslavlia i prigorodnykh territorii." November 26, 1991.

Malyi sovet Iaroslavskogo oblastnogo sovet narodnykh deputatov. "Reshenie No. 198 ob otchete predsedatelia komiteta po upravleniiu gosimushchestvom po ispolneniiu programmy privatizatsii gosudarstvennykh i munitsipal'nykh predpriiatii Iaroslavskoi oblasti na 1992 g. ot 30 sentiabria." September 30, 1992.

———. "Reshenie No. 231 o klassifikatsii avtomobil'nykh dorog v Iaroslavskoi oblasti, ot 26 fevralia 1992 g." February 26, 1992.

———. "Reshenie No. 234 o prodazhe zemel'nykh uchastkov pri privatizatsii imushchestva v oblasti." February 26, 1992.

Moskovskii gorodskoi sovet narodnykh deputatov. "Proekt: Osnovnye dokumenty po privatizatsii Moskovskogo gorodskogo zhilishchnogo fonda." Moscow, 1991.

"Postanovlenie Soveta Ministrov SSSR o general'nom plane razvitiia g. Leningrada." *Sbornik postanovlenii pravitel'stva SSSR,* 1966, no. 14: 275–82.

"Text of Rights Adopted by the Soviet Congress." *New York Times,* September 7, 1991, p. 5.

Tsentral'nyi komitet KPSS, Sovet ministrov SSSR. "O razvitii zhilishchnogo stroitel'stva v SSSR (Postanovlenie 31 iiulia 1957 g.)." *Arkhitektura SSSR,* 1957, no. 9: 1–6.

Index

153